James S. (James Samuel) Pollock

Resting places

A manual of devotion for private and family use

James S. (James Samuel) Pollock

Resting places
A manual of devotion for private and family use

ISBN/EAN: 9783742861580

Manufactured in Europe, USA, Canada, Australia, Japa

Cover: Foto ©Lupo / pixelio.de

Manufactured and distributed by brebook publishing software (www.brebook.com)

James S. (James Samuel) Pollock

Resting places

RESTING-PLACES.

By the Rev. JAMES S. POLLOCK, M.A.

THE PLAIN GUIDE. 100 pp. 32mo. Wrapper 2d. Cloth, 6d. 15th Thousand.

RESTING-PLACES. 176 pp. 24mo. Wrapper, 9d. Cloth, 1s. 6d. Bound with Book of Common Prayer, 2s. The Eight Parts in Tract form, 1d. each; 10d. per dozen.

WAYMARKS. 1d. each; 10d. per dozen:—
    1. *Set up Waymarks.* 2nd Thousand.
    2. *Baptized or Not?*
    3. *I Can't make it Convenient.*
    4. *The Real Presence.* 2nd Thousand.

Price 1d. each; 10d. per dozen:—

What Church Service must I attend? 10th Thousand.

What Ritual has God appointed? 8th Thousand.

Pastoral Advice of the Rev. John Wesley, M.A. 19th Thousand.

Prayers for Morning and Evening, on a Card. 2nd Thousand.

Romanising: a Lecture delivered in the Town Hall, Birmingham. 3d.

One Hundred Reasons against Auricular Confession and Priestly Absolution. With Answers. 3d.

RESTING-PLACES:

A MANUAL OF

CHRISTIAN

DOCTRINE, DUTY, AND DEVOTION,

FOR PRIVATE AND FAMILY USE.

"Thou in Thy mercy hast led forth the people which Thou hast redeemed: Thou hast guided them in Thy strength unto Thy holy habitation."—*Exodus* xv. 13.

LONDON: MASTERS, NEW BOND STREET.
OXFORD: MOWBRAY AND CO., ST. ALDATE STREET.
BIRMINGHAM: HODGETTS, CANON STREET.

1870.

BIRMINGHAM:
PRINTED BY WILLIAM HODGETTS,
CANON STREET.

PREFACE.

THE best apology for the appearance of this book is the fact that the "Plain Guide" came before it. A few simple Instructions under that title were published in November and December, 1867. A more complete edition followed in March, 1868. The rapid sale of the cheap edition, published in May, 1868, seemed to make it a duty to revise the book from time to time, that it might be less unworthy of the work it was doing. But, as frequent changes are inconvenient, the "Plain Guide" will, for the future, be published as nearly as possible in its present form.

Hence the need of the present work, which may perhaps contain what is most wanting in its predecessor, and supply a more complete manual of Christian Doctrine, Duty, and Devotion, for private and family use.

"Resting-places" will be found to contain in its first three "Parts" nearly all the Instructions and a great part of the Devotions of the "Plain Guide." The remaining five "Parts" are new, a few Chapters only having been published before.

In the sequel to a book which aimed at being very "Plain," there will naturally be many defects and more redundancies. "Resting-places" cannot hope to satisfy Christians who have been accustomed to the use of regular "Offices." But it may be a help to some who, while needing longer and more varied devotions than those of the "Plain Guide," find simple forms most useful to their souls.

"Resting-places" is chiefly compiled from English sources. Many of the best known and most valued forms of devotion have been, for that very reason, excluded. It seemed better to seek new and unfamiliar treasures, than to re-print what had already been edited so frequently and so well. This may account for the fact that the present work does not contain ten pages in common with any of the most popular books of devotion now in use.

Many of the hymns are new or unfamiliar, though a few favourites could not be passed by. My brother's verses, marked by his initials—T. B. P.—will, it is hoped, add to the usefulness of the book.

There is an apparent lack of intercessions marked as such. Those which seemed most important are added to the short forms of prayer arranged for private and family use in a week.

The book is divided into a number of short Chapters for the sake of more easy reference. Each "Part," however, is complete in itself, and is intended to supply a short manual of its subject.

The "form" and type of the book were chosen with a view to its being bound up with a convenient edition of the Book of Common Prayer; that its Instructions and Devotions might lead up to and prepare for the words of the Church.

JAMES S. POLLOCK.

Epiphany, 1870.

CONTENTS.

PART I.—FAITH AND DUTY.

	PAGE
1. Faith	17
2. The Creed	17
3. Devotions on the Creed	19
4. Hope	21
5. Prayer	21
6. The Lord's Prayer	22
7. Devotions on the Lord's Prayer	22
8. Charity	23
9. The Ten Commandments	24
10. Devotions on the Ten Commandments	25
11. Sacraments	27
12. Holy Baptism	29
13. Infant Baptism	29
14. Private Baptism	30
15. Adult Baptism	31
16. Renewal of Baptismal Vows	32
17. Confirmation	33
18. Renewal of Confirmation Vows	36
19. Sign of the Cross	37
20. Seven Gifts of the Spirit	37
21. Twelve Fruits of the Spirit	38
22. Four Cardinal Virtues	38
23. Feasts and Fasts	39
24. Three Good Works	39
25. Works of Mercy	39
26. Counsels	39
27. Growth in Grace	39

PART II.—REPENTANCE.

		PAGE
28.	Sin	41
29.	List of Sins	43
30.	Self-Examination	46
31.	Confession	48
32.	Absolution	49
33.	Going to Confession	50
34.	How to go to Confession	52
35.	A General Confession	54
36.	Prayers of Penitence	56
37.	Seven Deadly Sins	57
38.	Hymns	60

PART III.—HOLY COMMUNION.

39.	Going to Church	65
40.	The Real Presence	66
41.	Sacrifice	68
42.	Companion to the Altar	69
43.	Hymns	74
44.	Spiritual Communion	76
45.	Going to Communion	77
46.	How to go to Communion	78
47.	Before and After Prayer	80

PART IV.—ALL THE DAY LONG.

48.	The Morning	81
49.	The Day	83
50.	Hours of Prayer	86
51.	Morning Prayers	87
52.	Second Morning Prayers	88
53.	Nine o'Clock	88
54.	Twelve o'Clock	89
55.	Three o'Clock	90
56.	Evening Prayers	91
57.	Late Evening Prayers	91
58.	The Evening	92

PART V.—DAILY PRAYERS FOR A WEEK.

		PAGE.
59.	SUNDAY MORNING	97
60.	SUNDAY EVENING	98
61.	MONDAY MORNING	98
62.	MONDAY EVENING	99
63.	TUESDAY MORNING	99
64.	TUESDAY EVENING	100
65.	WEDNESDAY MORNING	101
66.	WEDNESDAY EVENING	101
67.	THURSDAY MORNING	102
68.	THURSDAY EVENING	102
69.	FRIDAY MORNING	103
70.	FRIDAY EVENING	104
71.	SATURDAY MORNING	104
72.	SATURDAY EVENING	105
73.	ACTS OF DEVOTION	106
74.	RULE OF LIFE	108
75.	SPECIAL PRAYERS	109

PART VI.—FAMILY PRAYERS FOR A WEEK.

76.	SUNDAY MORNING	113
77.	SUNDAY EVENING	114
78.	MONDAY MORNING	115
79.	MONDAY EVENING	115
80.	TUESDAY MORNING	116
81.	TUESDAY EVENING	117
82.	WEDNESDAY MORNING	118
83.	WEDNESDAY EVENING	119
84.	THURSDAY MORNING	119
85.	THURSDAY EVENING	120
86.	FRIDAY MORNING	121
87.	FRIDAY EVENING	121
88.	SATURDAY MORNING	122
89.	SATURDAY EVENING	123
90.	EIGHT BLESSINGS	124
91.	GOSPEL LESSONS	125
92.	LITANY FOR EVERY NEED	126

PART VII.—THE CHANGES OF THE WORLD.

		PAGE
93.	PROSPERITY	129
94.	ADVERSITY	129
95.	VARIOUS TRIALS	129
96.	RIGHT USE OF TRIAL	130
97.	FRIENDS IN TROUBLE	131
98.	TROUBLES OF THE NATION	131
99.	FOR ALL THAT ARE IN TROUBLE	131
100.	HYMNS	132
101.	VARIOUS PRAYERS	134
102.	CHILDBIRTH	136
103.	SICKNESS	136
104.	THOUGHTS FOR THE SICK	138
105.	HYMNS	140
106.	RECOVERY FROM SICKNESS	143
107.	THOUGHTS ON RECOVERY	144
108.	FOR ONE WHO IS DEPARTING	148
109.	FOR THE DEPARTED	149
110.	EPITAPHS	151
111.	IN ALL CHANGES	152

PART VIII.—THE SEASONS OF THE CHURCH.

112.	DIVISIONS OF TIME	153
113.	THE YEAR	153
114.	THE FOUR SEASONS	153
115.	THE MONTH	155
116.	THE WEEK	156
117.	THE DAY	157
118.	HARVEST	157
119.	ADVENT	158
120.	EMBER DAYS IN ADVENT	159
121.	CHRISTMAS	159
122.	CIRCUMCISION	160
123.	EPIPHANY	160
124.	SEPTUAGESIMA	161
125.	LENT	161

		PAGE
126.	Hymn	162
127.	Ember Days in Lent	163
128.	Holy Week	163
129.	Maunday Thursday	163
130.	Good Friday	164
131.	Eastertide	166
132.	Rogation Days	166
133.	Ascensiontide	166
134.	Whitsuntide	168
135.	Ember Days in Whitsuntide	169
136.	Trinity Sunday	169
137.	Ember Days in September	169
138.	Litany of God Incarnate	169
139.	The Blessed Virgin	170
140.	The Holy Angels	171
141.	The Holy Apostles	171
142.	The Holy Martyrs	171
143.	Feast of All Saints	171
144.	The Church	172
145.	Peace and Unity	173
146.	Revival	173
147.	Spiritual Gifts	174
148.	Home Missions	174
149.	Foreign Missions	174
150.	For Myself	175
151.	For my Friends	176
152.	For all Men	176
153.	Thanksgiving	176

HYMNS AND LITANIES.

[*Single Verses, and lines inserted merely as aids to memory, are not mentioned in this list.*]

	PAGE.
All hail, Redeemer of Mankind	74
As every night lays down our head	95
As we tread life's dreary journey	134
Before the door of every heart	62
Blessed Angels! while we silent lie	94
Blest be Thy love, dear LORD	93
Blest thought! He *now*, Who wept at Lazarus' grave	133
By the picture of Thy Passion	74
Come Holy Ghost, our hearts inspire	168
Come thou weary wandering child	60
Draw me, my Saviour, gently lead	133
Father, if Thou willing be	142
Forth in Thy Name, O LORD, I go	82
GOD of GOD, for man decreed	169
Go forth, my soul, another day	83
Holy JESU! I have crowned Thee	63
How can I seek Thy Presence, O my GOD	62
In GOD the Father I believe	19
JESU, Life of those who die	159
JESU, lover of my soul	141
JESUS treads the floor of Heaven	75
Loving Saviour hear me	60
My soul and body faint with pain	140
Now it belongs not to my care	142
O LORD, on Whom alone I rest	162

	PAGE
O may my Guardian, while I sleep	94
Omnipresent God, Whose aid	95
Open thine eyes, my soul, and see	81
Our Father Which in Heaven art	22
Pilgrim, are you heavy laden	85
Rock of Ages! cleft for me	141
Said I not so, that I would sin no more	93
Saviour most loving, bending before Thee	64
Shine on our souls, Eternal God	85
Spirit of love be in our heart	38
Taught by Temperance, we abstain	38
Thou shalt have no more Gods than me	25
Time himself, with all his legions	153
We believe, O Lord, In Thee	126
We pray for wisdom more and more	37
What time, my soul, sad thoughts prevail	133
Why should I fear the darkest hour	86
With all the powers my poor soul hath	74
When in the night I sleepless lie	95
When languor and disease invade	143
When pleasure shines upon my way	132

To the Reader.

"*He, that presents the following Papers to
"thee, designs to teach thee, as the Church
"was taught in the early Days of the Apos-
"tles, to believe the Christian Faith, and
to understand it; to represent plain Rules
"of good Life; to describe easy Forms of
"Prayer; to bring into your Assemblies
"Hymns of Glorification and Thanks-
"givings, and Psalms of Prayer. By
"these easy paths they lead Christ's little
"ones into the Fold of their Great Bishop.
"And if by this any Service be done to
"God [or man] it is hoped that God will
"accept it. And it is Reward enough, if
"by my Ministry God will bring it to pass
"that any Soul shall be instructed and
"brought into that State of good things,
"that it shall rejoyce for ever.

"But do thou pray for him that desires
"this to thee, and endeavour it."

INTRODUCTION.

To serve GOD is to reign: to work for GOD is to rest. This is our privilege: may it be our experience!

We commonly describe the Christian Life as a race, a strife, or a journey. So Holy Scripture speaks of it, and so it is. But our statements are incomplete. We have to keep in mind that the Christian race and its prize save us from a more wearisome course of sin,—that the Christian's strife and his victory take the place of a more severe struggle, whose only end would have been defeat and death,—that the Christian in his journey has already come to Mount Sion and to JESUS. If toil is the lot of the righteous, "there is no peace to the wicked."

PART I. Faith is the first Resting-place of the soul. We know nothing of the unseen, till GOD supplies that knowledge, giving us faith to receive it. In faith we rest, and are no more unsettled by any private opinions of our own. The teaching of GOD in His Church is our guide. Believing in JESUS we find rest unto our souls. In the Sacraments which the LORD commanded we have union with Him, receiving grace and power to do the will of GOD.

PART II. Many of us forget that we were purged from our old sins: backsliders even forget their Resting-place in the Church of GOD. The way of Repentance is the only way of return: each step, painful though it be, is a foretaste of rest, and is itself a refreshing after the weariness of sin.

PART III. The restored soul finds pasture. The Sacramental Presence is its stay. When GOD reveals Himself in the Resting-place prepared for His worship, then the sinner's heart rejoices and his cup is full.

PART IV. To dwell in the House of the LORD for ever is the aspiration of the soul that has truly seen GOD in His Sanctuary. We go on from strength to strength,—the Bread of Heaven our Food, the unwearying song of Heaven our Rest.

PART V. Morning and Evening, at the least, we must present ourselves before the LORD. However distracted by the cares of this life, we can begin and end our daily toil by a few heart-prayers of yearning and searching for the Resting-place above.

PART VI. The voice of joy and health is in the dwelling of the righteous. Each family will go apart, morning and evening, to rest awhile in the service of GOD.

PART VII. Every change and trial may be made a time of refreshing and a place for the weary to rest in. Hearts fixed upon true joys in the future, have quietness and confidence now.

PART VIII. We are resigned to the changing seasons of our mortal life, when we learn our share in the unvarying plan of eternity. The summer and winter of the Christian year help us to be sober on the bright days and calm on the dark days of our earthly pilgrimage. The life which we live in the flesh may have its joys and sorrows; but their sunshine and their shadows pass away. Our true life is hid with CHRIST in GOD. The Feasts and Fasts of His Church draw our hearts away from our own things, leading us to take up the Cross and follow Him. And those quiet Resting-places seem to mark the stages of the way by which we go to the many mansions of our Father's Home.

PART I.—FAITH AND DUTY.

" Come unto Me, all ye that labour and are heavy laden, and I will give you Rest."—S. Matthew xi. 28.

1.—FAITH.

FAITH is the first thing that a Christian needs. It is a gift of GOD, by which we are made able to believe all that GOD has told us. Your faith must be *firm*, because it rests on GOD, who cannot lie. Your faith must be *entire*, because it does not rest on your own private opinion. Your faith must be *active*, for faith without works is dead. Nothing must make you give up your faith. You must not choose your own religion; but believe all the truth that GOD teaches in His Church. The chief truths of the Christian faith are in

2.—THE CREED.

1. I believe in GOD the Father Almighty, Maker of heaven and earth:
2. And in JESUS CHRIST, His only Son, our LORD;
3. Who was conceived by the Holy Ghost, Born of the Virgin Mary,
4. Suffered under Pontius Pilate; was crucified, dead, and buried;
5. He descended into Hell; the third day He rose again from the dead;
6. He ascended into Heaven, and sitteth on the right hand of GOD the Father Almighty;
7. From thence He shall come to judge the quick and the dead.
8. I believe in the Holy Ghost;
9. The Holy Catholic Church, the Communion of Saints;
10. The Forgiveness of Sins;
11. The Resurrection of the Body;
12. And the Life everlasting. Amen.

This is the Gospel that all Christians must believe:—

I. GOD the Father made all things. In six days He made this world; and put Adam and Eve, the first man and woman, in the Garden of Eden. There the devil tempted Eve to eat of the fruit of a tree that GOD had told them not to touch. So GOD was angry at this sin, and by sin came death—not the death of the body only, but also the death of the soul for ever in Hell. But GOD so loved the world that He sent His Son to save sinners.

II. God the Son came to save all men. To do this He WAS MADE MAN. He had no Father on earth, but was conceived by the Holy Ghost. The Blessed Virgin Mary was His Mother. He was born at Bethlehem on Christmas Day, was brought up at Nazareth, and worked as a carpenter with S. Joseph, who was thought to be His father. When He was twelve years old, He stayed in the temple at Jerusalem, though S. Joseph and His mother knew not of it, and talked with the teachers of the law. When Jesus was about thirty years old, He was baptized by S. John the Baptist in the river Jordan; and was forty days in the wilderness tempted by the devil, yet without sin. He then went about doing good for three years and a half. He taught the people as God only could teach them, cast out devils, healed the sick, and raised the dead. All this time He was a poor man and a man of sorrows, not having even a place to live in. His twelve Apostles whom He had chosen, and some other faithful people, were with Him. At last, Judas, one of the twelve, betrayed His Master. Jesus gave Himself up to those that wished to kill Him. He suffered many things from His enemies on that sad night: they scourged Him, and spat upon Him, and struck Him, and put a crown of thorns upon His head. The next morning, on Good Friday, He suffered under Pontius Pilate, the Roman governor of the country; being nailed to a cross on Mount Calvary, near Jerusalem. Two thieves were crucified with Him, one on His right hand and the other on His left. There our Blessed Saviour died, giving up His spirit into His Father's hands, and going into the place of the dead. Joseph of Arimathea buried Him in his own new tomb. The Sacred Body of Jesus did not decay; but He rose again on the third day, Easter Day, and showed Himself to His disciples and other witnesses. He stayed on earth forty days, telling the Apostles what they were to do when He left them, promising that the Holy Ghost would come to them. He went up to heaven on Ascension Day. He is in heaven now with His Body and pleads for us; and loves us as much as when He died to save us. He will come again some day to earth, and will judge us all, both the living and the dead. To those who are not ready to receive Him, He will then say, "Depart, ye Cursed," and to those that are ready He will say, " Come, ye Blessed."

III. God the Holy Ghost makes all Christians holy.

He first came to the disciples on Whitsunday, ten days after JESUS had ascended. Then the Church of CHRIST was formed. That Church is one, for CHRIST is one. It is holy, for the Holy Ghost is in it. It is apostolic, for it is built on the twelve Apostles. It is Catholic or universal, for it holds all the faith, and has in it all GOD's people. There is a Communion of Saints; for all the holy ones, both the living and the dead, are one: they love and pray for one another. There is one Baptism for the Remission of Sins. It is by Holy Baptism that we are made members of CHRIST, and have all our sins washed away. And there is Pardon of Sins for those who fall after Baptism; if we confess our sins, we may have the gift of Absolution. We shall all rise again with our bodies. And that we may rise to glory, we must live in CHRIST and on CHRIST, while we live upon the earth. JESUS said, "I am the Bread of Life;" and just before He suffered on the cross He gave us the Blessed Sacrament of His Body and Blood, that we might eat and live for ever. We must all live for ever, either in Heaven or Hell. But JESUS said, "Him that cometh to me I will in no wise cast out." He has "opened the kingdom of heaven to all believers." Therefore we say at the end of our Creed "Amen;" meaning that we believe all that is in it, and that we hope through the Gospel to be saved.

These are the chief things that the Creed teaches us. We learn by it that there are Three Persons in One GOD, and that all Three are equal in all things—also that They all equally love us, and desire to do us good.

3.—DEVOTIONS ON THE CREED.

In GOD the Father I believe,
First of the Trinity,
Whose word created all that is
In heaven, and earth, and sea—
In JESUS CHRIST, His Son, our LORD,
By Holy Ghost conceived,
Of Mary born, by Pilate slain,
Derided, disbelieved;
Who on the third day rose from death,
Ascended into heaven;
And sits at GOD's right hand of power
Till judgment shall be given.
I in the Holy Ghost believe,
One Holy Catholic Church.
The blest Communion of the Saints,
Free grace for all who search.
And I believe in sins forgiven,
In rising from the dead,
In life for ever, joy in heaven,
Or woe in hell instead.

A. J. B.

I believe; LORD, increase my faith; and give me grace

that, with a holy life, I may adorn the religion I profess. Keep me stedfast in this faith into which I have been baptized, that no errors may separate me from Thee. May Thy love, O merciful Father; Thy grace, O blessed JESUS; Thy fellowship, O Holy Spirit, defend and comfort me, till I attain the end of my faith, even the salvation of my soul. Amen.

LORD, I believe; help Thou mine unbelief, and supply the defects of my weak faith.

Grant me to love the Father for His tender love, to adore the Almighty for His power, to commit the keeping of my soul to my faithful Creator.

Grant me to partake from JESUS of salvation, from CHRIST of Anointing, from the only-begotten Son of Adoption; that I may serve the LORD for His Conception, in faith; for His Birth, in humility; for His Sufferings, in patience and hatred of sin; for His Cross, in crucifying all beginnings of sin; for His Death, in killing the desires of the flesh; for His Burial, in burying evil thoughts by good works; for His Descent, in meditation upon hell; for His Resurrection, in newness of life; for His Ascension, in setting my heart on things above; for His Sitting on High, in minding the good things on His right hand; for His Second Advent, in awe of His return; for His Judgment, in judging myself before I am judged.

Grant me from the Holy Spirit to receive the breath of saving grace; that in the Holy Catholic Church I may have my calling, holiness, and portion; with a Fellowship of her sacred rites and prayers, fastings and mournings, watchings, tears, and sufferings; for assurance of Forgiveness of sins; for hope of Rising and passing to eternal Life. Amen.

[*The* 31 *Prayers in Chapters* 3, 7, *and* 10 *are arranged for use in a month.*]

1. Glory be to Thee, O Father, Who didst make all things, and Who didst so love the world, as to give Thine only Son to save us.

2. Thou, O Blessed JESUS, art the only Son of GOD, full of grace and truth: in Thee sinners have hope: all love, all glory be to Thee.

3. LORD JESUS, Thou didst stoop so low as to take our nature, having GOD only for Thy Father, and Mary, a pure virgin, for Thy Mother; and didst dwell among us to save us: all love, all glory be to Thee.

4. O Blessed JESUS, my LORD and my GOD, may I grieve for my sins, which

grieved Thee; may I love Thee for suffering and dying for sinners, who caused all Thy griefs: O may I always love Thee! O may I never grieve Thee more!

5. All praise and glory be to Thee, LORD JESUS, Who didst taste of death, and take away the sting of death; Who didst rise again, and give us the victory.

6. Glory be to Thee, LORD JESUS, Who didst ascend to heaven, and there pleadest for us sinners. Let my affections rise to Thee, and return to the earth no more.

7. Glory be to Thee, LORD JESUS, Who from Thy throne at GOD's right hand wilt come to judge the living and the dead: may I ever be mindful of the strict account I have to give.

8. All love, all glory be to Thee, O Blessed Spirit, the Giver of life: may I never grieve Thee, and may Thy Presence never depart from me.

9. O my GOD, keep me always in the fold of the Catholic Church, that so I may never be taken away from Thee, but with Thy saints may praise and love Thee.

10. All love and glory be to Thee, O GOD, Who dost pardon sinners that repent. GOD be merciful to me a sinner.

11. Glory be to Thee, O GOD, Who dost now raise sinners from the death of sin, Who wilt raise the bodies of Thy saints and give them glory.

12. O Thou great Author and Finisher of our faith: increase in me all Christian graces, and make me to be numbered with Thy saints in glory everlasting.

4.—HOPE.

After faith the next virtue that a Christian needs is hope. Hope is a gift of GOD. It is built on the promises of CHRIST, on His merits, and on the mercy of GOD, Who will give us the help we need. We are not to hope or trust in ourselves, or in our own good works. We cannot do anything good, except by the grace of CHRIST working with us. Do not sin by *presumption*, or think that GOD will pardon you, whether you do good or evil. Do not sin by *despair*, or think that GOD has given you up, and will not save you. If you have hope in GOD, it will lead you to

5.—PRAYER.

All real Christians pray. It is a very sad thing for any one who calls himself a Christian to live without prayer.

When you pray, think well of what you are going to do. Think of your own weakness and sin. Think of GOD's power and goodness. Kneel down humbly, and keep in mind that you are in the presence of GOD. Take care how you speak to GOD. Do not let your thoughts wander, or your eyes see what may disturb you. Speak slowly and with reverence; and ask GOD's help, that you may pray aright. The best of all prayers is

6.—THE LORD'S PRAYER.

The Address.

Our Father, Which art in Heaven.

Seven Petitions.

1. Hallowed be Thy Name.
2. Thy Kingdom come.
3. Thy will be done in Earth, as it is in Heaven.
4. Give us this day our daily bread.
5. And forgive us our trespasses, as we forgive them that trespass against us:
6. And lead us not into temptation;
7. But deliver us from evil:

The End.

For Thine is the Kingdom, the Power, and the Glory, For ever and ever.
Amen.

This prayer was given to us by our Saviour JESUS CHRIST. We must use it when we pray; and all our prayers ought to be like it. We speak to GOD as our heavenly Father, because He is the Father of our LORD and Saviour JESUS CHRIST. In the first *three* prayers we ask for grace that GOD's Name may be honoured, that all may know and serve Him as their King, and that all may give up their own wills, and do His will. Then we say *four* prayers for ourselves. First, we ask for the food that keeps soul and body in life. Sin kills the soul, but we go on to pray that GOD would in mercy forgive us, help us in temptation, and keep us from evil. Lastly, we give glory to GOD, Who lets us pray to Him; and say "Amen," which here, and at the end of all other prayers, means, "So be it!" or, "May GOD grant what we ask!"

7.—DEVOTIONS ON THE LORD'S PRAYER.

Our Father Which in Heaven art; LORD, Hallowed be Thy Name.
Thy Kingdom come: Thy will be done in Earth and Heaven the same.
Give us our daily bread for soul and body day by day;
As we forgive our debtors, so forgive our debts we pray.
Into temptation lead us not; from evil keep us free;
For Thine the Kingdom, Power, and Glory are eternally.

[*See Note before the* 12 *Prayers in Chapter* 3.]

13. O Father Almighty, let my soul rise up to Thee, when I pray, in heavenly thoughts and desires and love. Draw my heart away from earth, when I speak to Thee in heaven.

14. O LORD GOD, may Thy Name be confessed, Thy greatness and goodness be adored for ever in our hearts, our mouths, and our lives. Let every thing that hath breath praise the LORD.

15. O my GOD, let it be Thy good pleasure to put an end to sin and sorrow, pain and death; that all who wait for Thy salvation may for ever love and praise Thee in Thy kingdom of glory.

16. LORD, Thy will and Thy laws are holy, just, and good. Give me grace, like the blessed spirits above, to will what Thou willest, to will because Thou willest, to will as Thou willest, and to will when Thou willest.

17. Give me, O heavenly Father, my daily bread, and with it give me Thy blessing. Above all, give me the Bread of Life, the Bread that came down from heaven, the Body and Blood of Thy most Blessed Son, to feed me unto life eternal.

18. For Thine own mercies' sake, and for the merits of the Son of Thy love, forgive me, O my Father, and forgive all penitent sinners. Glory be to Thee, O LORD, Who, to teach us charity, hast made our forgiveness of others the condition of obtaining Thine.

19. LORD, Thou knowest how weak I am, and how ready my deceitful heart is to yield to the tempter; O be merciful to me, save and help and deliver me; keep me ever on my guard; and give me the victory at last.

20. O Father of mercy, save me from the evil that tempts me, from the evil of sin, the evil of punishment, the evil one, the evil world, my own evil heart, and all things that may lead me to do what displeases Thee.

21. To Thee, O LORD GOD, do I pray, for Thine is the kingdom over all; on Thee do I rest, for Thine is the power to help and bless me; to Thee I offer up my praises, for Thine is the glory for ever and ever. Amen.

8.—CHARITY.

There are three great Christian virtues—Faith, Hope, and Charity; but, S. Paul tells us that "the greatest of these is Charity." When we believe all that GOD has taught us, our faith leads us to hope in His mercy. When we have faith and hope we love GOD, Who is so great and good. And JESUS CHRIST has said, "If ye love Me, keep My commandments."

O that I, with Faith and Hope,
And with Love surrounded,
In the dreadful Judgment Day
May not be confounded!

9.—THE TEN COMMANDMENTS.

The First Table.

I. Thou shalt have none other gods but Me.

II. Thou shalt not make to thyself any graven image, nor the likeness of any thing that is in heaven above, or in the earth beneath, or in the water under the earth. Thou shalt not bow down to them, nor worship them: for I the LORD thy GOD am a jealous GOD, and visit the sins of the fathers upon the children, unto the third and fourth generation of them that hate Me, and shew mercy unto thousands in them that love Me, and keep My commandments.

III. Thou shalt not take the Name of the LORD thy GOD in vain: for the LORD will not hold him guiltless that taketh His name in vain.

IV. Remember that thou keep holy the Sabbath day. Six days shalt thou labour, and do all that thou hast to do; but the seventh day is the Sabbath of the LORD thy GOD. In it thou shalt do no manner of work, thou, and thy son, and thy daughter, thy man-servant, and thy maid-servant, thy cattle, and the stranger that is within thy gates. For in six days the LORD made heaven and earth, the sea, and all that in them is, and rested the seventh day; wherefore the LORD blessed the seventh day, and hallowed it.

The Second Table.

V. Honour thy father and thy mother; that thy days may be long in the land, which the LORD thy GOD giveth thee.

VI. Thou shalt do no murder.

VII. Thou shalt not commit adultery.

VIII. Thou shalt not steal.

IX. Thou shalt not bear false witness against thy neighbour.

X. Thou shalt not covet thy neighbour's house, thou shalt not covet thy neighbour's wife, nor his servant, nor his maid, nor his ox, nor his ass, nor anything that is his.

These Ten Commandments of GOD teach us two things—our duty towards GOD, and our duty towards our neighbour. The first *four* teach us to love GOD above all for His own sake. The last *six* teach us to love all men as ourselves for GOD's sake, and to do unto all men as we would they should do unto us.

Our duty towards GOD is to believe in Him as the only

true GOD, to worship Him aright, to honour His Holy Name and His Word, and to serve Him truly all the days of our life. Our duty towards our neighbour is to give due honour to all men, to hurt nobody by evil thought or word or deed, to keep our bodies pure, to be honest in all our dealings, to speak kindly and truly of all, and to desire nothing wrong.

By keeping these Commandments we do our duty, not only to GOD and man, but also to ourselves. When we sin against any of these Commandments we must humbly ask GOD to have mercy upon us, and to lead our hearts to keep His laws.

10.—DEVOTIONS ON THE TEN COMMANDMENTS.

1. Thou shalt have no more GODS but Me.
2. Before no idol bow thy knee.
3. Take not the Name of GOD in vain;
4. Nor dare GOD's Holy Day profane.
5. Give both thy parents honour due.
6. Take heed that thou no murder do.
7. Be pure in thought, and word, and deed;
8. Nor steal, whatever be thy need.
9. Make not a wilful lie, nor love it.
10. What is Thy neighbour's do not covet.

LORD, make me understand Thy Law,
Show what my faults have been;
And from Thy Gospel let me draw
Pardon for all my sin.
     Amen.

LORD REMOVE FROM ME

1. Impiety and profaneness, superstition and hypocrisy.
2. Worship of idols and of persons.
3. Rash oaths and irreverence.
4. Neglect of worship and indevotion.
5. Pride and carelessness.
6. Strife and wrath.
7. Uncleanness and intemperance.

LORD GIVE ME

1. Piety and godliness.

2. Acceptable worship and service.

3. Sound speech and reverence.

4. Diligence and devotion.

5. Humility and obedience.
6. Charity and patience.
7. Purity and soberness.

8. Idleness and deceit.	8. Contentedness and liberality.
9. Lying and slandering.	9. Truth and uprightness.
10. Every evil notion, impure thought, and base desire.	10. Good thoughts and perseverance to the end.

Make me to go in the path of Thy Commandments; for therein is my desire. I have gone astray like a sheep that is lost: O seek Thy servant, for I do not forget Thy Commandments.

[*See Note before the 12 Prayers in Chapter 3.*]

22. O my GOD, let nothing take away my heart from Thee. May I have no other GOD, no other love, but only Thee.

23. O my GOD, make me so zealous for Thy honour, that I may try to worship Thee as I ought, and may show a due regard to all the parts of Thy worship.

24. O my GOD, let it be the great business of my life to love and glorify Thy Name with my lips and in my life, and by leading all I can to honour Thee.

25. O my GOD, give me grace to worship Thee at all times, in private and in Thy holy temple; and to serve Thee truly all the days of my life.

26. O my GOD, help me for Thy sake to give due honour to all those set over me, those placed under my charge, and all with me at home and at work, in the Church and in the world.

27. O my GOD, teach me to seek the health, safety, and happiness of my neighbour; that he may be the better able to serve and love Thee.

28. O my GOD, let Thy love make me hate all uncleanness, that I may purify myself as Thou, LORD, art pure.

29. O my GOD, teach me to be just in giving to all men what is due to them. Help me to be thankful to Thee for Thy gifts, temperate in my use of them, and liberal in giving to those that are in need.

30. O my GOD, give me grace always to speak the truth, and to hate all things that hurt my neighbour's good name.

31. O my GOD, give me a heart that may, for the love of Thee, stop all the risings of sinful desire, before they lead to consent or to any evil words and deeds.

The LORD JESUS said—

1. Thou shalt love the LORD thy GOD with all thy heart,

and with all thy soul, and with all thy mind, and with all thy strength.

2. Thou shalt love thy neighbour as thyself.

On these two commandments hang all the law and the prophets.—*S. Mark.* xii. 30, 31. *S. Matt.* xxii. 40. Compare *Deut.* vi. 5, x. 12.

1. With all thy soul love GOD above.
2. And, as thyself, thy neighbour love.

First Table—Commandments
I–IV.

O GOD, Who alone art worthy of my love: Grant me grace, that I may never forget Thee nor Thy glorious perfections; but serve Thee according to Thy Word, and according to my vows, in sincerity and godly fear: that I may not spend Thy holy days in idleness or in formal acts of worship, but may honour and serve Thee with my body and my spirit; through JESUS CHRIST my Saviour. Amen.

Second Table—Commandments
V–X.

Open mine eyes, O LORD; that I may see Thy law to be holy and just and good; and that I may keep it with my whole heart. Teach me to love and honour all whom Thou hast placed over me; to do violence to no man; to hate all uncleanness, deceit, lying, and evil desires; for JESUS CHRIST'S sake. Amen.

Golden Rule.

The LORD JESUS said—

All things whatsover ye would that men should do to you, do ye even so to them; for this is the law and the prophets.—*S. Matt.* vii. 12.

Be you to others kind and true,
As you'd have others be to you;
And neither do nor say to men
Whate'er you would not take again.

11.—SACRAMENTS.

We cannot believe or do as we ought without GOD's help. So GOD has given us His Holy Sacraments as means of grace. JESUS CHRIST was made man, and thus became the Saviour of all that come to Him: He now applies that salvation to each through Sacraments.

I. By HOLY BAPTISM we are washed from the sin of our birth, and born again of water and of the Spirit.— Chapters 12–16.

II. HOLY COMMUNION feeds us with the Most Precious Body and Blood of our Saviour JESUS CHRIST.—Part III.

Holy Baptism and Holy Communion are the two great Sacraments of the Gospel, appointed by CHRIST Himself, necessary for all Christian people. They stand above all other ordinances in the Church of GOD.

3. *Confirmation* gives us the

Holy Ghost to strengthen us.—Chapters 17–18.

4. *Absolution* cleanses us from sins committed after Baptism.—Chapter 32.

5. By the ministry of GOD's Priests in the *Visitation of the Sick* our souls are helped in their affliction.

6. By *Holy Orders* we are provided with Divinely-appointed Ministers.

7. *Holy Matrimony* blesses and sanctifies the state of the married.

———

The Visitation of the Sick is described in S. James v. 14. 15. Sick people ought to send for a clergyman before they are too weak to receive the full benefit of his help. The visit of a clergyman does not condemn a sick man to death: "the prayer of faith" may even "raise him up." Sickness is "GOD's visitation:" the priest comes on GOD's behalf to help the afflicted to make his peace with GOD, or to minister to him according to the special needs of his soul. [*Prayers for the Sick*, Part VII.]

The Prayer Book contains services for making, ordaining, and consecrating Bishops, Priests, and Deacons. The Deacon assists the Priest, the Priest celebrates all the Offices of the Church except Ordination and Confirmation, which are reserved for the Bishop only. The clergy of the Church of England trace their descent from the Apostles whom the LORD JESUS ordained. The Bishop of Rome, a few years ago, sent some Bishops to England; but, of course, it would be a sin for us to give up the clergy whom GOD has set over us, and follow the Roman clergy or any other teachers of religion who try to make converts.

In Holy Matrimony a Christian man and woman are "joined together by GOD;" and JESUS said, "What, therefore, GOD hath joined together let not man put asunder." *S. Mark* x. 9. Some irreligious people like to be "without GOD" in their marriage; and the Registrar gives them a license to live together as man and wife. They think in this way to escape public disgrace; but theirs is not *Holy* Matrimony. Church people should not marry in Advent or Lent, or during Great Festivals.

The services used in the celebration of the Sacraments and other Ordinances are found in the Book of Common Prayer. In the title-page of that book you will see that we have the services "of the Church," that is, of the *one Church* of CHRIST; we have them "according to the use" of the *branch of that*

Church which is planted in this land. A great part of the Prayer Book is very ancient. Its forms of worship have been handed down from the early Church. "The use" of the Church of England was arranged very much in its present form in the year 1549. Since that time the Prayer Book has been revised: it was put forth, just as we have it now, by the authority of the Church of England, in the year 1662. Some people, who do not believe Church doctrine, want the Prayer Book altered again; and they blame the clergymen who obey the Prayer Book as it is. Alterations of that kind would be very sinful. For "the use" of the Church of England must agree with the doctrine of "the Church" of which it is a part. 1 *Cor.* xi. 16.

12.—HOLY BAPTISM.

The first Sacrament is that by which we first come to JESUS. This is what the Bible says to you—"As many of you as have been baptized into CHRIST have put on CHRIST." *Gal.* iii. 27. Therefore, of course, as many as have not been baptized have *not* put on CHRIST, and are none of His. All baptized persons are Christians, though they are not all good Christians. But no unbaptized persons are Christians, though they may be trying to do what is good. All baptized persons are children of GOD, though they are not all obedient children. But no unbaptized persons are children of GOD, though they may do some things that GOD's children do. This seems quite plain. We cannot save ourselves, or make ourselves GOD's people. It must be GOD's act, and He has taught us that He does it in Holy Baptism. We must be born again. We can't be saved by our own good thoughts, or feelings, or faith. JESUS CHRIST is our only Saviour, and we must come to Him to be saved. Therefore "repent and be baptized, every one of you." *Acts* ii. 38. You *must* come to your Saviour in this way. and not in any other way of your own. Hear His words, "Verily, verily, I say unto thee, Except a man be born of water and of the Spirit, he cannot enter into the kingdom of GOD." *S. John* iii. 5.

13.—INFANT BAPTISM.

Infants must be baptized as soon as possible after their birth. It is very wrong to put off this duty, as some people do, for months or even years. JESUS said, "Suffer the little children to come unto Me, and forbid them not." *S. Mark* x. 14. "Registration" is not Baptism. Registration means only that the infant has been born into this world—"born in sin:" Baptism means that in it the infant has been born *again* of water and of the Spirit. Baptism is more than "naming." The Christian name is only a sign of the new birth into God's family, just as the surname is a sign of the infant's birth into its parents' family. Names that are really "Christian" can be chosen from the Church Kalendar. Infants ought to be baptized publicly, that is, in Church during the service; that the people may be reminded of their own Baptism, and may pray for the children. The office for the "Public Baptism of Infants" ought not to be used in Church as a private service, when there is not a public service going on. It is the duty of every Christian to do all he can to bring infants to Holy Baptism, and to take care that no infants die without this blessing. It is not necessary for either father or mother to be present at the Baptism of their child. The mother should be Churched as soon as she can go out. No fee should be given to any one for baptizing a child, or writing its name in the registers.

Christian people ought to be glad to act as sponsors for their friends' children, when asked to do so. Some persons are afraid to do this; for they think they shall have to answer for the children's sins. This is a great mistake. All that God-fathers and God-mothers have to do is to help parents in the care of their children's souls, by seeing that the children are taught their duty to God and man. You will find all this explained in the end of the Baptismal Service. It is the duty of parents and God-parents to train up children " in the nurture and admonition of the Lord." It is a great sin for Church people to neglect the teaching of their children, or to send them to any but Church Schools, where they will be trained up in the religion into which they have been baptized.

The Rules of the Prayer Book allow "dipping" or "pouring." They do not say anything about "sprinkling" infants or adults.

14.—PRIVATE BAPTISM.

When an infant is in danger of death, but not otherwise, the priest should be asked to baptize it privately. If there is not time to get a priest, any man or woman may baptize, being careful to pour clean water on the infant, and to say, while pouring it, the Christian name, with these words—"I baptize thee in the name of the Father, and of the Son, and of the Holy Ghost. Amen." Infants baptized privately are truly and perfectly baptized, if *water* and *the right words* are used; and they must not be baptized again. But, if a child so baptized gets well, it must be taken to Church to be publicly "received into the Congregation of CHRIST'S flock," and signed with the sign of the cross.

Common sense as well as religion tells us that only children that have had Christian Baptism can have Christian Burial. Those only who were given to GOD in His appointed way when they were alive can be committed to His care when they are dead.

15.—ADULT BAPTISM.

If you were not baptized when a child, you must not put off that necessary Sacrament. Do not say that you won't be baptized, because you are not good enough. The question is, do you *wish* to be better than you are? Whether you are what is called bad or good, the blessings of Holy Baptism may be yours, if you only seek them with all your heart. Pray to GOD to forgive your past neglect, and to guide you now.

Your parish clergyman will help you in your preparation. Don't wait for him to find out that you are unbaptized; but go to him as soon as you can, and don't be afraid to tell him yourself.

Before Baptism you must read, if you can, the Service for the "Public Baptism of such as are of riper years, and able to answer for themselves." You will find it in the Prayer Book, just before the Catechism. The title of the Service tells you what it means. You are now "of riper years;" and, as you have lived some years in the world, you have many stains of sin on your soul. You were born in sin; and you have, more or less, lived in sin. You are now coming to Holy Baptism to have all those sins washed away in your Saviour's Precious Blood, and to be received into His Church as a child of GOD. You have to "answer for yourself;" so you must know all you can about the religion of CHRIST. The Church Catechism will help you in this. The Creed will tell you what you must believe; the Ten Commandments will show you what you must do; the LORD'S Prayer will teach you how GOD lets His children pray to Him; and everything in the Catechism will help you to know the great gift that GOD would grant you, and the need of seeking it well. Read the four questions in the Baptismal Service that you will have to answer when you come to be baptized; and be ready to profess your faith as one that truly desires to live a godly life.

At the time of your baptism, come with prayer and fasting, and think of nothing but of the blessing you seek. For it is GOD that grants it to you, and the priest only acts for GOD. Think of the Baptism of your Saviour—how the heavens were opened, and the Spirit descended like a dove, and the voice of the Father said, "This is my beloved Son, in whom I am well pleased." *S. Matt.* iii. 16, 17. This tells you what to hope for. The gates of heaven are shut against sinners; but the Son of GOD has opened them to all believers who confess Him as you are doing. Pray for the baptism of the Spirit. Pray that GOD may own you as His child, and be well pleased with you always.

After baptism, do not forget that you "have been purged from your old sins." Guard well the gift of GOD, and try to live the life of a Christian. Read *Eph.* ii. 1-5, and *Col.* i. 10-18. You have now a right to say the LORD's prayer, and to call GOD your Father.

16.—RENEWAL OF BAPTISMAL VOWS.

The grace of Holy Baptism comes only once. Nobody who has been baptized as an infant can be baptized again. It is a great sin to repeat the Sacrament in any case. Yet it is well to keep in mind the blessings of Holy Baptism. You may from time to time renew your vows, and ask GOD to stir up His gift in you.

When you do this, go to your Father in secret, and think of the time when he first made you His child at the Holy Font. You were born in sin, but then you were new-born of water and of the Spirit. How pure you were when GOD thus cleansed you! Think of this, and think also of your sins. Think how often you have broken your vows, and stained your soul. Then, meekly kneeling on your knees, tell GOD of your longing to have revived in your soul the grace of Holy Baptism, and to make a solemn resolve to live up to your Christian profession. Then say solemnly and thoughtfully—

In the name of the ✠ Father, and of the Son, and of the Holy Ghost. Amen.

Our Father. [*Say the Lord's Prayer.*]

I renounce the devil and all his works, the vain pomp and glory of the world, with all covetous desires of the same, and the carnal desires of the flesh, so that I will not follow nor be led by them.

I believe all the Articles of the Christian Faith.

I will try to keep GOD's Holy Will and Commandments.

I heartily thank my heavenly Father, that he hath called me to this state of salvation, through JESUS CHRIST my SAVIOUR. And I pray unto GOD to give me His grace, that I may continue in the same unto my life's end.

I thank Thee, O Lord, for my birth, but chiefly for my new birth in Holy Baptism. Let me not forget the object of my birth, nor depart from the blessing of my baptism. Let me ever keep the state of grace and salvation that Thou hast given me; and if by sin I ever fall from it, let me by repentance rise again to it. Lord, who gavest me this life on earth: grant me a better life with Thee in heaven; for His sake, whose Birth, Life, and Death make all ours blessed, JESUS CHRIST our LORD. Amen.

This devotion may be used at any time. It is good to use it on the Feast of the Epiphany, Jan. 6, when the Church tells you of CHRIST's Baptism; on Easter-Eve and Whitsun-Eve, the days that used to be set apart in the Church for the baptizing of converts; on the anniversary of your own Birth or Baptism; on the Feast-day of the Saint whose name you may bear; when you are present at a baptism of infants or adults; after any fall into sin, or after receiving any great mercy from God.

17.—CONFIRMATION.

When you were fed as an infant, you did not know anything about the way food kept you alive. When you were baptized as an infant, you did not know anything about the way Baptism gave you new life. It was the duty of those that loved you to see that you were fed and baptized, simply because both were for your good. Because you were fed as an infant, and so kept alive, you have to take your place in the world, and work for yourself. Just in the same way, because you were baptized as an infant, and made a Christian, you must take your place in GOD's Church, and live a Christian life. In your Catechism you have often been asked the question, "Dost thou not think that thou art bound to believe and to do as they [your God-parents] have promised for you?" and you have said, "Yes, verily; and by God's help so I will."

From this you learn three things:—

1. Confirmation is not a taking upon yourself of vows by which your God-parents were bound, for they were never bound by your vows. You were bound by the vows made at your baptism: they only promised to have you taught the promise *you* had made by them.

2. Confirmation is not a mere renewal of your baptismal vows, for as we saw in Chapter 16, you may do that as often as God's grace leads you to it, without the help of Bishop or Priest.

3. The only *new* thing that Confirmation binds you to is to confess CHRIST "openly before the Church," as the preface to the Confirmation Service says.

Now that you see what you are to do, let me show you what you are to get from God in Confirmation. Holy Baptism gave you life; Confirmation gives you strength. In Holy Baptism you were born of water and of the Spirit: in Confirmation you seek more grace to bring forth the fruits of the Spirit. This is the real meaning of Confirmation. You must not think too much of what you do yourself, but rather of the good work of God upon your soul.

From all this you will see the strange mistake that some people make, when they put off Confirmation till they grow up. They think that they have to learn a great deal, and be very good before they are confirmed. All the while they forget that Confirmation means strengthening; and that it is the young, and the weak, and the tempted that most need that grace. Nobody, who is in earnest, is either too young or too old to be confirmed. In the early Church, Confirmation used to come close after Baptism in the case both of infants and grown-up people. It is a very good thing for children to give themselves early to God. How many might be saved from sin and woe, if they had God's strengthening grace before they went out into the world and were tempted to sin! But if you have not been confirmed in your early days, there is all the more reason why you should not put it off any longer. No matter how old you are: God will receive you. Young people have the promise, "Those that seek Me early shall find Me." You must hear God's voice saying to you, "It is time to seek the LORD."

Of course it is a very solemn thing to come to Confirmation, but it is a very sad thing not to come when GOD calls; for JESUS said—"Whosoever therefore shall confess Me before men, him will I confess also before My Father Which is in Heaven. But whosoever shall deny Me before men, him will I also deny before My Father Which is in Heaven." *S. Matt.* x. 32, 33.

You will be taught by the Priest what to do before you come to be confirmed. You will read in the Bible how people, who had been baptized by a Minister, afterwards were confirmed by Apostles; and will see why the Bishop comes to lay his hands on you. *Acts* viii. 5, 12. 14, 15. The chief thing is to examine yourself. The Clergyman will help you in this part of your preparation.

On the day of Confirmation don't think too much of your dress: let it be neat and plain. Be silent and thoughtful when you go to Church. Be careful to join in the service. Say "I do" clearly, and as if you meant it. Receive the laying-on of hands with meekness and faith, bowing down your head in adoration. Remember that it is GOD that acts by the Bishop.

After Confirmation hear GOD'S voice saying to you— "Thou, therefore, My son, [or, My daughter] be strong in the grace that is in CHRIST JESUS."— "Be thou faithful unto death, and I will give thee a crown of life." 2 *Tim.* ii. 1; *Rev.* x. 2. Read also *Gal.* v. 16-25, and *Eph.* vi. 10-18.

If you cannot be confirmed soon, you may come to the Holy Communion if you are "ready and desirous to be confirmed." [See Rubric at the end of the Confirmation Service.] If you have been confirmed, and have not received the Holy Communion afterwards, you have committed a great sin. Read Part III. and speak to your Clergyman.

Before Confirmation.

My Father in Heaven: Thou hast been pleased to make me Thy child in Holy Baptism, and to give me Thy grace. I bless and glorify Thee for all that Thou hast done for me from the day of my Baptism until now. I desire to come to Confirmation, because it is Thy will and my duty; but I mourn over my sins, which have made me so unworthy of Thy favour. Grant, I pray Thee, most merciful Father, that, when I come to Confirmation, Thy Holy Spirit may give me strength to conquer my evil habits, to resist temptation, to obey Thy laws, and to become a good soldier of JESUS CHRIST.

LORD JESUS, cleanse me in Thy Precious Blood, and take away all my stains.

O Divine Spirit, prepare me for Thyself. I come to give myself to Thee, that Thou mayest live and reign in me for ever. Amen.

[See Chapters 20, 21, 133.]

After Confirmation.

O my GOD, I desire to praise and adore Thee for all that Thou hast done for me, and chiefly for the blessing of Confirmation. May Thy Holy Spirit guide and rule my heart in all things, driving away all that may profane Thy temple. Arm me for the war, stand by me in my conflicts, and crown me with victory at last; for JESUS CHRIST's sake. Amen.

[See Chapters 20, 21, 134.]

18.—RENEWAL OF CONFIRMATION VOWS.

The grace of Confirmation is only given once. If you have been confirmed, you cannot be confirmed a second time. But you may have the grace of Confirmation revived in your soul, and may renew your vows.

To do this you must see how far you have used the grace given to you at your Confirmation, and how far you have been a good soldier or a coward under the standard of the Cross. Then confess the wrong that you have done, and renew your purpose of fighting against the enemies of your soul; praying for the strength and help of the Holy Ghost, without Whom you can do no good thing. Lastly, say, on your knees, the following devotion—

In the name of the + Father, and of the Son, and of the Holy Ghost. Amen.

Our Father, [*Say the Lord's Prayer*]

Strengthen me, I pray Thee, O LORD, with the Holy Ghost the Comforter, and daily increase in me Thy gifts of grace; the spirit of wisdom and understanding; the spirit of counsel and strength; the spirit of knowledge and true godliness; and fill me, O LORD, with the spirit of Thy holy fear, now and for ever. Amen.

Let Thy fatherly hand, I beseech Thee, O LORD, ever be over me; let Thy holy Spirit ever be with me; and so lead me in the knowledge and obedience of Thy Word, that in the end I may obtain everlasting life, through our LORD JESUS CHRIST. Amen.

[See Chapters 20, 21, 134.]

This devotion may be used at any time. It is good to use it on Whitsunday, when the Holy Ghost came down upon the Apostles; on the Anniversary of your own Confirmation; as often as you are present at a Confirmation, or when there is one in your neighbourhood; when you are greatly tempted to sin, or tried in any other way; when you have fallen into any sin or danger.

19.—SIGN OF THE CROSS.

Every infant that is baptized is signed with the sign of the cross, in token that he "shall not be ashamed to confess the Faith of CHRIST crucified." For this reason, among others, we use the sacred sign. When we use it with the Invocation—"In the Name of the + Father, and of the Son, and of the Holy Ghost. Amen"—it forms a short Creed, meaning that we believe in Three Persons in One GOD, and that all our hope is in JESUS, Who died on the Cross. We ought not to be ashamed of our faith, or of this way of declaring it. You can sign yourself by making a line with your right hand from your forehead to your breast, and another line from your left shoulder to your right. The sacred sign is a defence against temptation, especially against evil thoughts. It may be used at the beginning and end of your prayers, and before you commence any work of importance or difficulty. But it is very wrong to use the sign in a formal way, or to wear a cross or crucifix as a mere ornament. A crucifix is a cross with a figure of our Saviour upon it. *S. John* iii. 14, 15.

Ashamed of JESUS! Yes, I may
When I've no guilt to wash away,
No tear to wipe, no good to crave,
No fears to quell, no soul to save.

20.—SEVEN GIFTS OF THE SPIRIT.

Isaiah xi., 2.

O Holy Spirit of Grace, be Thou my Wisdom, to teach me my faith;—my Understanding, to teach me my duty;—my Counsel, in all my doubts;—my Strength, against all temptations;—my Knowledge, in what belongs to the state of life to which I am called;—my Godliness, in all my actions;—my Fear, all the day long.

We pray for *Wisdom*, more and more
To know the GOD our hearts adore;
For grace to *Understand* and feel
The truths Thou dost to faith reveal;
For *Counsel* to be wise and true
In judging what is right to do;

For *Ghostly Strength* to meet the foe,
And bear with courage toil and woe;
For *Knowledge* to direct our will
To choose the good and shun the ill;
For *Godliness*, like GOD to be,
In truth, and love, and purity;
For *Holy Fear*, to watch and pray,
And keep within the narrow way.
T. B. P.

21.—TWELVE FRUITS OF THE SPIRIT.

Gal. v., 22. 23.

Spirit of *Love*, be in our heart,
And make us loving as Thou art;
And grant us holy *Joy* to find
In loving GOD and all mankind;
So in our hearts Thy *Peace* be known,
And in our lives its power be shewn;
In days of trial make us strong
To bear our cross and *Suffer long*;
Give *Gentleness* in heart and mind,
A voice and manner always kind;
And may our inward feeling lead
To *Goodness* shewn in word and deed;
May we in *Faith* on GOD rely,
And judge our neighbour hopefully.

In *Meekness* may our hearts be still,
And yield to all our Father's will.
And may we, strong in *Patience*, bear
What GOD may send of grief or care.
May *Modesty* of thought ensure
That all our lives be *Chaste* and pure.
May *Temperance*, with careful rein,
And *Continence* our flesh restrain.
T. B. P.

22.—FOUR CARDINAL VIRTUES.

Taught by *Temperance* we abstain
   From all less for greater goods:
Slighting little drops we gain
   Full, and sweet, and lasting floods.

Armed with *Fortitude* we bear
   Lesser evils, worse to fly:
Mortal death we do not fear,
   Lest we should for ever die.

Justice we observe by giving
   Every one his utmost due;
That, in peace and order living,
   All may freely heaven pursue.

Prudence governs all the rest;
   Prudence makes us still apply
What is fittest, what is best,
   To advance great charity.

23.—FEASTS AND FASTS.

Every Sunday is a Feast of the Resurrection: every Friday is a Fast of the Passion. Our LORD JESUS CHRIST is the Sun that rules our seasons: the Christian year follows the events of His life on earth. On Fast Days, when you deny yourself in food, you ought not to go to any place of amusement. You will find a list of the Feasts and Fasts in the Church Kalendar. [*Devotions for the Seasons of the Church, Part VIII.*]

24.—THREE GOOD WORKS.
S. Matt. vi. 3. 5. 17.

Fasting He doth and *Giving* bless,
And *Prayer* can much avail;
Good vessels all to draw the grace
Out of salvation's well.

25.—WORKS OF MERCY.
Corporal Works.
1. To feed the hungry.
2. To give drink to the thirsty.
3. To clothe the naked.
4. To shelter the stranger.
5. To visit the sick.
6. To minister to prisoners.
7. To bury the dead.
S. Matt. xxv. 34–40.

Visit, give drink, give meat, redeem the slave:
Clothe, tend the sick, and lay the dead in grave.

Spiritual Works.
1. To warn sinners.
2. To teach the ignorant.
3. To counsel the doubtful.
4. To comfort the afflicted.
5. To bear with the weak.
6. To forgive injuries.
7. To pray for the living and the dead.

Gal. vi. 1; *Dan.* xii. 3; *S. James* v. 20; *Rom.* xii. 15; *Rom.* xv. 1; *S. Luke* vi. 37; *S. James* v. 16.

Counsel, rebuke, instruct in wisdom's way:
Console, forgive, endure unmoved, and pray.

26.—COUNSELS.
1. Poverty. *S. Matt.* xix. 21.
2. Chastity. 1 *Cor.* vii. 37, 38.
3. Obedience. *S. Mark* i. 16–20.

Christian Duties are binding on all who have been baptized. Counsels of Perfection are for those who are called to them. Great care should be taken lest anyone refuse a call from GOD, or attempt what GOD has not appointed for him. All religious vows are voluntary; and only after long trial are they made perpetual.

27.—GROWTH IN GRACE.
"Thou art not able to do these things of thyself, nor to walk in the Commandments of GOD, and to serve Him

without His special grace," (Catechism).

Signs of Grace and of its growth.

1. Love to GOD, His people, His ordinances.
2. Christian humility and self-denial.
3. Tenderness of conscience, watchfully resisting sin.
4. Meekness under injuries, and resignation to the will of GOD.
5. Concern for the welfare of the Church, and for the salvation of all.

Hindrances.

1. Sinful companions and amusements.
2. Pressure of worldly business carried on according to the customs of the world.
3. Any person or pursuit loved more than GOD.
4. Religious controversy, and lack of Christian converse.
5. Giving up a duty, or going back to a sin.
6. Formal worship, and neglect of private prayer.
7. Prosperity and the praise of man.

Helps.

1. Meditation and self-examination.
2. Habitual watchfulness, self-denial, and prayer.
3. Frequent Communion, and a constant sense of the Presence of GOD.
4. The Bible, with other books of instruction and devotion.
5. Christian Work, especially among the sick and the poor.
6. Church Services, and Christian fellowship.
7. Seasons of sorrow and retirement.

Perseverance.

It is not enough to begin what is right: we must go on and persevere to the end. To do this we must be humble, not trusting in ourselves, trusting in GOD only, trying to do GOD'S will, asking and seeking GOD's help. 1 *S. Peter* v. 10, 11.

PART II.—REPENTANCE.

"My people hath been lost sheep—they have forgotten their Resting-place."—*Jeremiah* 1. 6.

28.—SIN.

SIN is the worst thing in the world. There are two kinds of sin—the sin of our birth and the sin of our life.

1. The sin of our birth comes to us from our first father Adam. GOD made man pure and good like Himself. But Adam fell into sin, and all his children are sinners too. Every child is born in sin, and must be born again of water and of the Spirit. The sin of our birth is taken away by our new birth in Holy Baptism. When we are baptized, we are made members of the Church, which is the Body of CHRIST, the Second Adam. This makes us children of GOD, and heirs of heaven.

2.—The second kind of sin is the sin of our life. The sin of our birth is taken away by our second birth, but its mark is on us still. Though we are made Christians, our bodies are weak, and we must die like other men. Our souls are weak too; and they will die again, if GOD's grace does not keep them in life. Sin is the sickness that kills the soul. Men go astray "as soon as they are born."—*Ps.* lviii. 3. "There is none that doeth good, no not one."—*Ps.* xiv. 2. No man is free from sin. "In many things we offend all."—*S. James* iii. 2.

Three great enemies lead us into sin—the devil, the world, and the flesh.

1. The devil led our first parents astray; and he now goes about to devour us. We have to fight against the devil and his angels.

2. The world is against us too. It leads us wrong by its follies and vanities. Bad people in the world want to make GOD's people as bad as they are. Everyone has trials of this kind.

3. Worst of all, the flesh is against us. The devil and his angels go about to kill us, and come to us with their temptations. Bad people seem nearer to us than the devil: the world is around us always, and it is not easy to escape it. But the greatest danger is within us. We all have evil hearts. So, when GOD's Holy Spirit would make us pure, the flesh, our evil nature, works against Him. Our sin-

ful desires are very strong, and it is hard to keep them down.

We sin in three ways—in thought, word, and deed.

1. A bad thought is one that brings to our mind a thing which it would be wrong to say or do. If you drive away the thought as soon as you know it to be sinful, you do not stain your soul, but gain a victory. When a bad thought comes back again and again, but you fight against it each time till you beat it back and get rid of it, then you gain a far greater victory. It is wrong to dwell on a bad thought as if listening to it, to take any kind of pleasure in it, or to be slow in driving it away, even though you do not let it stay long. And, when you give consent to the thought of sin, or carry it out in word or deed, your sin is then greater than before. You must guard your heart. Wrong thoughts lead to wrong words and deeds.

2. It is very hard to keep from saying what is wrong. Most people talk a great deal too much. And when the heart is full of sin, the lips will shew it.

3. Wrong acts come from wrong thoughts and words. When we have sinned with our hearts or our tongue, we make our guilt far worse by going on to *do* what is wicked.

There is another way of marking our sins. Some people think that they will be saved, because they do nobody any harm. But this is not enough. You must let GOD guide your thoughts, words, and actions. You must "cease to do evil," but you must also "learn to do well." You sin—

1. When you think, say, or do anything wrong.

2. When you are slow in thinking, saying, or doing anything right.

You see now that it is a sin *not* to do your duty.

You ought to try to do all parts of your duty to—

1. GOD. 2. Your neighbour. 3. Yourself.

There is one thing that ought to be kept in mind always—the great evil of sin.

1. Every little *venial* sin, no matter how small you may think it, does you great harm. It spoils the good work of GOD in you. It stains and weakens your soul.

2. If you do not take care, venial sins will lead to *mortal* sins—I mean, you will be tempted to sin wilfully against GOD in greater things; and will be led to wicked deeds that will take away the life of your soul. If you grieve the Holy Spirit, He may leave you. If GOD's grace and help are lost on account of your sins, then your soul must die.

The sins called mortal or

deadly, with the virtues most unlike them, are these:—

Deadly Sins.	Opposite Virtues.
1. Pride.	1. Humility.
2. Covetousness.	2. Liberality.
3. Lust.	3. Chastity.
4. Anger.	4. Meekness.
5. Gluttony.	5. Temperance.
6. Envy.	6. Charity.
7. Sloth.	7. Diligence.

The chief thing you have to do is to try to find out the sins that most beset you. Most likely your worst sin is one of the seven deadly sins. You will find all the chief forms of those sins in the list of sins against the Ten Commandments, which is given in the next Chapter.

You have another danger to flee. Even when you think that you are not doing anything wrong, you may sin by having share in the sin of others. This you may do in nine ways—

1. Telling any person, whom you may have in your power, to do anything wrong.

2. Advising any person, whom you may be able to guide, to do anything wrong.

3. Setting a bad example, which others may follow.

4. Giving your consent to anything sinful.

5. Permitting sin that you might have stopped.

6. Taking part of what is got by sin.

7. Hiding sin or sinners.

8. Defending sin or sinners.

9. Saying or doing anything to excite others to sin.

Above all things take care to avoid, as far as you can, all persons, places, and occasions that are likely to lead you into sin. Many people, who are afraid to sin, take pleasure in *going near* sin. Then they excuse themselves by saying that the temptation was too strong. Beware of this. "GOD is not mocked." Read Psalm L.

29.—LIST OF SINS.

[*The List of Sins follows the order of the Ten Commandments of God, which are given in Chapter* 9.]

I. Loving any person or thing more than GOD—pleasing yourself instead of doing the will of GOD—trusting in your own strength instead of in the help of the Holy Ghost—setting up your private judgment above the truth which GOD teaches in His Church—unbelief and doubt—talking idly to scoffers and profane persons — denying your religion through fear of man—reading profane books and lending them to others—doing what conscience tells you is wrong—not thanking GOD when things go well with you—not trusting in GOD—complaining against GOD in trial, sorrow, and loss—forgetting GOD's presence—thinking lightly of sin—giving up hope of GOD's mercy—not making haste to repent, when you have fallen into sin.

II. Not going regularly to Church—going to places of worship other than the Church of England—looking about you, whispering, talking, and laughing in Church, either in time of service, or before and after it—leading others to do wrong things in Church—not attending to the service, but letting your thoughts and eyes wander to other things—not bowing, kneeling, and standing at the proper times—doing these and other such things for people to see you—being afraid of getting laughed at for shewing reverence at Church, or to holy things—laughing at others for what you think their reverence or want of reverence—not asking the advice of GOD's Priest, or not going to Confession when you need it—not being present at Holy Communion on Sundays and other Holy-days, when you can come—going out of Church before the Communion Service is over—not receiving Holy Communion at stated times—receiving It without due preparation—leaving out your private prayers, morning or evening—saying your prayers without praying—not kneeling at prayer—fortune-telling.

III. Saying GOD's Holy Name in common talk, and in a light way—quoting the Bible without reverence—speaking evil of GOD, and despising holy things—speaking idly or carelessly of Holy Baptism, Confirmation, Confession, and Holy Communion; or talking lightly of GOD's Saints, and of the Ceremonies of the Church—talking too much about religious questions, or about your own religious feelings—acting the hypocrite—going through religious services in a formal way—taking GOD's Name in vain by not acting according to the Christian Name and profession of your Baptism—breaking your Baptismal and Confirmation Vows, or any promises made to GOD in sickness and at any other time—making a careless or imperfect Confession.

IV. Doing work on Sundays that might be done at other times—buying and selling on Sundays; or spending the day in sleeping, walking with careless people, idleness, worldly pleasure, and sin—staying away from Church for slight reasons—not keeping Feasts and Fasts, such as Ascension Day and Good Friday—wasting your time—not trying to serve GOD truly all the days of your life.

V. *Children.* Not showing love and respect to your parents—doing forbidden things—not doing what you are told to do—doing things without leave or taking things without leave—not helping your parents in trouble, sickness, and old age—speaking rudely to them, and speaking undutifully of them to others—not praying for your father and mother, and all set over you—playing truant—idleness at school — want of respect to your pastors and masters—giving needless trouble.

Parents. Unjust partiality—not having your children baptized soon after their birth—not teaching them to say their prayers, and to do their duty to GOD and man—not sending them to a Church School on Sundays and Week-days, if they need it—letting them go into bad company, and wander about in the evenings—not warning them against sin, setting them a bad example, or in any other way letting them go into the way of temptation—ill-using them or spoiling them — spending on yourself the money needed for your family—not praying for your children.

All. Not giving due honour to all men—not keeping in mind your duty to those set over you, the Church and the Clergy, the Queen and other rulers, your employers and helpers — choosing a place of work where your faith or good character may be lost, and obeying man rather than GOD through false shame—not following the advice of your pastor—selfishness—unkindness—rudeness.

VI. Anger in thought, word, or deed—hastiness of temper—abuse—threats—revenge, or desire of it—sullenness—fretfulness—wishing harm to anyone—making others angry by harsh and rude words or actions—insult—tyranny—cruelty to animals—quarrelling or leading others to quarrel—doing harm to the souls of others by bad example, bad books, or bad company—not trying to do good to others.

VII. Thoughts, desires, looks, words, and actions against modesty and purity, either with others or when GOD only sees you—leading others into impurity, and going yourself in the way and in the sight of it, even when you do not intend to sin—speaking lightly of what is impure—using or lending bad books and pictures—boldness of manner, words, dress, and looks—vanity—being fond of dress and admiration—eating and drinking more than is good for you—talking and thinking too much about food—not saying Grace at meals—sleeping too much—giving way to idleness and sloth, neglecting your work, not denying yourself, and not keeping the Fasts appointed by the Church,

VIII. Stealing, cheating, receiving and keeping what was stolen—buying and selling unfairly—taking part in theft, fraud, and injustice; or wishing to do so—wasting or injuring what belongs to others—wasting your employer's time, and doing your work badly—following an unlawful trade, or trading unlawfully because others do so—buying things without intending to pay—carelessness in business — breaking promises and agreements — helping others to do anything dishonest — letting others take what is in your charge—not giving back what you have got dishonestly to the person wronged. or to his heirs, or to the poor— not making amends, as far as you can, for any wrong done to any other — not paying taxes.

IX. Lies—the habit of adding to a story—making careless statements—false witness—speaking of the faults and defects of others without cause, and with pleasure — talking too much—gossipping—telling tales and secrets—being glad to think, hear, or speak evil of others — rash judgments—false promises—speaking so as to lead people to think that you know evil of anyone—helping others to speak against their neighbours by guessing and asking questions—not restoring the good name of anyone whom you have slandered—flattery, pretended friendship, and backbiting.

X. Discontent—complaining of your lot in life—peevishness—longing for riches, rank, or honour that others have—jealousy and envy—not trying to do your best where GOD has placed you—depending on others when you ought to learn and labour to get your own living—not giving what you can to GOD, and to His poor, for the benefit of the souls and bodies of men, for CHRIST's sake—stinginess—not denying your desires and will: not keeping under your body: not trying to make GOD's will the rule of your life.

30.–SELF-EXAMINATION.

It is not enough to say that you are a sinner like other people. Everybody will confess this. GOD asks you, "*What* is this that thou hast done?" *Gen.* iii. 13.

You are to examine yourself and not others. "Every one of us shall give account of *himself* to GOD." *Rom.* xiv. 12. Don't think of other men's sins. Seek cleansing for your own soul.

You ought not to put off this duty; for *delay*

1. Strengthens evil habits, and weakens your power of resisting them.

2. Shuts by degrees the door of GOD's mercy.

You cannot examine yourself without GOD's help. "The way of the wicked is as darkness: they know not at what they stumble." "There is a way which seemeth right unto a man, but the end thereof are the ways of death." *Prov.* iv. 19; xiv. 12.

Begin your self-examination by saying this prayer:

"How many are mine iniquities and sins? Make me to know my transgression and my sin." "Try me, O GOD, and seek the ground of my heart: prove me and examine my thoughts. Look well if there be any way of wickedness in me, and lead me in the way everlasting.' *Job.* xiii. 23; *Ps.* cxxxix. 23, 24.

Then think of yourself as a child of GOD, and of your wickedness in following the temptations of the world—the flesh—and the devil—sinning against GOD—your neighbour —and yourself—in thought— word—and deed—. Think not only of mortal sins—but also of venial sins—. Try to find out your worst and most easily-besetting sins — also whether you have helped any other to sin—. Notice in each case how far you sinned through ignorance—weakness —or wilfulness—. Chapters 28 and 29 will help you so far in your work.

You may go on to think of the places and company you have been in—your amusements and work—your waste of money, time, and talents— your temptations and sins in hearing, seeing, knowing, thinking, desiring, speaking, enjoying, keeping in mind anything against the law of GOD.

Some sins need to be carefully weighed—

1. The *person*, that is, yourself who offended; also those with whom, and against whom you offended.
2. The *matter* in or about which you sinned.
3. The length of *time* the sin was continued.
4. The nature of the *place*.
5. The *end* aimed at.
6. The *means* used.
7. The *number* of your relapses.
8. The *injury* done by the sin, in the way of damage, or scandal, or bad example.

Ask these questions:—
Who else? What? Where?
    How long?
Why? How? What times?
    What wrong?

Sorrow for Sin.

It is not enough to count up your sins. You will be truly sorry for sin, if you think seriously about it. For by your sins you have—

1. Offended against your Father in Heaven.

2. Slighted the work and renewed the sufferings of JESUS CHRIST your Saviour.

3. Grieved or quenched the Holy Spirit.

4. Made the devil and his angels glad.

5. Made the good angels sorry.

6. Lost the happiness of heaven.

7. Deserved the misery of hell.

8. Given scandal to the Church.

9. Helped and encouraged the wicked.

10. Forsaken the way of peace.

Do not trust in your own feelings, or expect to be saved by them. Do not vex yourself about the degree of your sorrow. But pray to GOD to help you to be sorry for sin as committed against Him, Who has been a kind, merciful Father to you. For this is contrition or "godly sorrow." It ought to—

1. Come from GOD as its Author.

2. Take in all your sins.

3. Make you hate sin above all things.

Turning from Sin.

Do not confound Regeneration and Conversion. Regeneration is GOD'S gift of the new birth in Holy Baptism, without works; Conversion is your turning away from sin to good works under the guidance of the Holy Spirit. Regeneration comes once and in a moment: Conversion need not have any definite beginning, may begin more than once, and is the work of a life-time. We die unto sin once: we kill sin every day, GOD calls upon all of us to repent, that is to forsake sin. "Godly sorrow worketh repentance to salvation."—2 *Cor.* vii. 9-11.

31.—CONFESSION.

Sin is the soul's disease. If you examine yourself, you will see how great your sin has been, and how sick your soul is.

When people feel a little sick, they try to cure themselves. To do this they take some medicine that has done them good before, and so may get relief. But when they find themselves very sick, and are afraid that they may die in their sickness, then they send at once for the doctor. When he comes, they tell him just how they feel. He looks at them, and tries to find out all that is wrong. He asks questions about what they have been doing, and how they are. And then he does his best to find out the right medicine to give them, tells them how they are to take it, and what they are to do in order that they may get well again.

How quickly people send for the doctor when they feel really ill! How eagerly they take his medicines, and follow his advice! How frightened people would be, if they knew that there was a dreadful disease attacking themselves, and every body round them, and that there were no doctors to visit the sick!

If you really feel your sin to be a dangerous disease, you will be anxious to see a doctor. I am glad to tell you that there is one very near you. Our Saviour JESUS CHRIST is the Physician of the Soul. He is your only hope. His Blood alone cleanseth from all sin. In it you may wash, and be clean. He said "Him that cometh unto Me, I will in no wise cast out." You must keep this truth in your heart —that you are not saved by any feelings of your own, but by the medicine that is given to heal you. If, then, you penitently confess your sin to GOD, humbly asking to be forgiven for CHRIST'S sake; and if you pray to be guided by GOD'S Holy Spirit in leading a new life, your prayer will be heard. No priest on earth can do you any good, and no prayers of your own can be of any use, except all be done in the Name of the LORD JESUS.

Our Saviour is gone into Heaven, but He still hears and helps us. We read in the Bible that He has left His ministers in the world to heal His people with the medicine which He has given to them. He "hath given to us the ministry of reconciliation." 2 *Cor.* v. 18. So, if you feel yourself to be a great sinner; if you want help to examine yourself; if you want to know what your sickness is, and how you may be healed—in this case don't let these good thoughts leave you, but go to some clergyman, and ask his advice. When you go, take care that you do not deceive him, but tell him all that is on your mind. Go to the clergyman just as you would go to the doctor—I mean, try to let him know what is wrong with you, being sure that you tell the worst part of your disease. He will teach you how to make a good Confession.

32.—ABSOLUTION.

Good advice is all very well in its place, but it is not medicine. When people only fancy themselves ill, it may be enough for the doctor to go and cheer them up, speaking comfortable words; and telling them that they are not so bad as they thought, but that, by taking care of themselves, they will soon be quite well again. Or, when people are only delicate and weak, it may be enough even in this case for a doctor to give them good advice as to food, exercise, and such things, telling them how to guard against diseases that threaten. But when people are really ill and in danger, the doctor perhaps does not talk so much, but he does far more. He knows that good advice won't cure his patient, so he applies the proper remedies.

Just so is it with your soul and its disease. If you only fancied yourself a sinner, or were only in danger of falling into sin for the first time, it might do for the clergyman to give you good advice, shewing you how to take comfort and rejoice in GOD'S love to you. But sin, you know, is not a mere fancy: it is a very dreadful and a very real thing. So the physician of the soul does more than comfort you. He points you to the fountain open for sin, and tells you of the Precious Blood of JESUS. He urges you to come to JESUS and wash away all your stains. He tells you also of a way by which you may have that Blood applied to your soul. As you were washed from your sins in Holy Baptism, you may be washed again by the Absolution spoken to you in GOD'S Name by His Priest. But I shall say more to you about this in the next Chapter.

33.—GOING TO CONFESSION.

Many people in these days wish very much to go to Confession, and to receive Absolution; but they cannot quite make up their minds to do so. Two things, for the most part, keep them back. They don't like Confession, and they don't know the value of Absolution. A few words on each of these points may be of use to you.

I. You don't like Confession. But, before you make up your mind against it, think of these things—

1. GOD told the Jews to confess to their Priests. *Lev.* v. 5. *Numb.* v. 6, 7.

2. When our LORD sent His ministers to remit and retain sins, He did not mean that they should do this unjustly or carelessly, without knowing the sins of the people. *S. John* xx. 23.

3. The Prayer Book, in the first Exhortation to Holy Communion tells the people to "open their grief" to their own Priest, or to some other, as often as they "cannot quiet their own conscience." Have you up to this time, perhaps for many years after your Confirmation, not gone to Holy Communion? Then your conscience cannot safely be quiet; and when by GOD'S grace you are "grieved and wearied with the burden of your sins," you should "open

your grief." On the other hand, are you preparing for Communion with a quiet conscience? Why is your conscience quiet? Is it because you are without sin, or because you are asleep?

4. The "Visitation of the Sick" tells the priest to "move" the sick man to "a special confession of his sins, if he feel his conscience troubled with any weighty matter." Healthy people have souls to be saved as well as sick people. Are you troubled? If so, make your confession. If not, is it because there is no weighty matter, or because you do not feel it and are not "weary and heavy laden."

5. You have done without confession so far; but you might do better, if you had this means of grace?

6. People may laugh at you, if you go to confession; but angels will rejoice over you, if you penitently seek any help that your soul needs.

7. It is better to be ashamed here than to be condemned hereafter.

8. GOD's Priest is a sinner like yourself. He now knows that you and he are sinners: after confession he may know you as a pardoned sinner. The clergy go to confession as well as the laity.

9. GOD's Priest will not speak to any one about your sins. It would be a very great sin for him to do this. He knows very well that he would lose his soul if he broke the seal of confession.

10. Priests sometimes make mistakes. So do doctors and lawyers; yet we go to them, when our lives and estates are in danger. Do you value your soul? Do you believe that it is in danger?

II. You don't know the value of Absolution. But think of these things:—

1. JESUS CHRIST healed a man sick of the palsy, that the people might know that "the Son of man hath power *on earth* to forgive sins." *S. Matt.* ix. 6. GOD gave "power *unto men*," v. 8.

2. JESUS CHRIST gave this power "*in earth*" (*S. Matt.* xxviii. 18) "*unto men,*" when He went into heaven—" As my Father hath sent Me, even so send I you.—" Receive ye the Holy Ghost: Whose soever sins ye remit, they are remitted unto them, and whose soever sins ye retain, they are retained." *S. John* xx. 21, 22, 23. *S. Matt.* xviii. 18.

3. The Church of England takes the words of JESUS just as they stand, not denying them nor explaining them away. So the same words are spoken to each Priest of the Church of England, when he is ordained—" Receive the Holy Ghost;—whose sins thou dost forgive, they are forgiven;

and whose sins thou dost retain, they are retained."

4. Every Christian must receive the Holy Communion. So every one, who cannot with quiet conscience receive It, must ask the help of GOD's Priest, that he may be able to obey GOD's law. One of the Exhortations, to the Holy Communion in the Prayer Book tells people that the use of "opening their grief" is that they "may receive the benefit of absolution," as well as advice.

5. The "Visitation of the Sick" in the Prayer Book tells the Priest to move the sick man to "a special confession of his sins," if his conscience is troubled, and gives an absolution that may be said after confession. Sick are often not so near death as other people that seem quite well. Do not trust to a death-bed repentance. "Live this day as if thy last." If your soul is sick, GOD's priest will not deny you absolution, because your body is not sick too. 2 S. Tim. iv. 2.

6. No man can forgive you your sins. Never forget this. The Priest only acts for GOD, as he does in Holy Baptism, when sin is first washed away. And it would be a great sin for the priest to absolve you, if GOD had not told him to do this. JESUS CHRIST is the One High Priest.

7. The LORD JESUS CHRIST would not have given this power of absolution to His priests, if He did not think it good or needful for His people. Does *your* soul need it?

One thing I must say to you before you read the next Chapter. You are not to think that a formal confession, made as a matter of duty, is enough. The blessings that GOD offers should be really *desired*. Nobody is urged to accept the gift before his heart is prepared for it. From this you will see the reason why the Church advises confession only to the "troubled," and offers absolution only to those that "desire it." (See "Visitation of the Sick.") You see what good reason the Church has for these cautions. For Absolution, like Holy Communion, is a blessing only to those prepared for it.

34.—HOW TO GO TO CONFESSION.

Many people have quite made up their mind that they ought to go to Confession, yet put it off. This is very wrong.

There can be no good reason for delay. If GOD puts a good thought into your heart, the sooner you carry it out the better. Go to your parish clergyman, or to some other priest who will help you, and tell him what you want. Listen to the advice he gives you, and then prepare yourself in good earnest for the gift that GOD offers you.

First Confession is the most important of all. So, if you have not been to confession before, you had better read this "Part." With the help given to you, look back upon the whole of your past life. To do this well you may have to divide your life into two, three, or even more parts, finding out the sins of one part after another.

If you have been to confession before, all you have to do is to look back upon the time that has passed since your last confession. But, if you think of any sins not before confessed, you should now confess them.

When you have done your best to find out your sins, you had better write out your confession, or at least notes of it, to use when you go to the priest. If you don't do this, you may be sorry to find that you have forgotten many things that you ought to have said.

You may make your preparation at home or in the Church, taking care that you give yourself enough time for the work. The last thing you must do is to kneel down humbly, and think of the wrong things you have to confess; adding some of the Devotions in Chapters 35—38, or others like them.

When you go to your confessor, keep in mind that JESUS CHRIST has sent him to you—that your Saviour knows the depths of your heart, and will Himself come to be your Judge. Kneel down, and think that you are at the feet of JESUS on His Cross, Who is ready to save you, and to wash you from your sins in His own most Precious Blood. When you see that the priest is ready, you may say, "Father, give me your Blessing, for I have sinned." When the blessing has been given, you may begin thus:—

I confess to Almighty GOD, before all the company of Heaven, and to thee, my father, that I have sinned very much, in thought, word, and deed, through my fault, through my own fault, through my most grievous fault. [Here you may "smite" your breast, if you like. *S. Luke* xviii. 13; xxiii. 48.] Especially I accuse myself that since my last confession, which was —— ago, I have—

Then name your sins fully, plainly, and humbly, in a clear voice, and not too fast. Speak to GOD all that is in your heart, as if it was the last time you were to ask for mercy. After you have done this, you may end with these words:—

For these and all the other sins of my life I am heartily sorry; I desire to amend my life; I humbly ask pardon of GOD, and of you, my father, penance, counsel, and absolution.

Listen to all that your priest says to you. Answer him with truth, and as plainly as you can. Be ready to do all that he tells you, and to follow his advice about keeping from sin. When the priest says the words of Absolution, receive the gift with a thankful heart, and hear JESUS saying to you some words of peace like these—"Thy sins are forgiven—go in peace—sin no more, lest a worse thing come unto thee." *S. Luke* vii. 48, 50. *S. John* v. 14.

Do not talk idly to others about your confession or theirs. It is a very great sin to trifle with serious things. But go and thank GOD for His mercy, and make good resolves.

35.—A GENERAL CONFESSION.

Father, I have sinned against Heaven and before Thee. I am no more worthy to be called Thy child.

But I am sorry for my sins. and I return to Thee. O cast not out my soul. Turn not Thy mercy from me. Thou hast been very good to me, Lord teach me to pray to Thee, and spare me now.

My GOD, I am vile, but I am thine. O save me, and despise not the work of Thine own hands. Thou LORD, didst take me out of the dust of the ground, and didst form me after Thine own image. Thou gavest me the breath of life, with all my powers of body and soul. Thou hast kept me in life, and saved me from many dangers even to this hour. LORD draw nigh unto my soul and save it.

In Thy great mercy Thou wast pleased to make me one of thy faithful and elect children, when I was born again in the waters of Holy Baptism. Then I was made Thine own. From that day Thou hast given me the power to serve and to love Thee. But I have grieved thy Holy Spirit, and sinned against Thy grace.

I confess that I have lost my purity, and provoked Thy anger. Yet I have been spared, while death has taken away many sinners in the midst of of the sins and follies of their youth. I sinned daily, and daily Thou didst wait to be gracious. I fled and Thou soughtest me. I wearied myself with sinning, and Thou wast not weary of bearing with me. How often have I been warned by words of love and deeds of kindness, by threats of anger, and by terrible judgments! Yet I have gone on in sin. I have used all my powers to offend Thee, and have even made the work of Thy hands to rebel against Thee. My feet have run to evil. My hands have been opened to covetousness. My eyes have gazed upon vanity. My ears have hearkened to lies. My heart has turned away from Thee. My affections have been set on things of the world. I have not thought of Thy law and of Thy commandments; but I have sought out ways of breaking them. Thou hast appointed all things to serve Thee; I have made use of them to offend Thee. Thou hast given me all things needful, that I might give them and myself to Thee; I have taken all to myself and robbed Thee. My health and strength have been used against Thee; yet Thou, in Thy mercy, hast moved the tongue that blasphemed Thee, governed the members that offended Thee, maintained the wretched sinner who, at Thy cost, served Thine enemies.

And Oh! my Father—greatest sin of all—I have taken occasion from the knowledge of Thy mercy to go on still in my wickedness. The means to destroy sin has been to me a motive of sinning. Because Thou art so good, I thought I might be wicked. Because Thou didst not punish my sins, I went on sinning. Because of Thy great benefits, I have committed against Thee great offences. I have abused Thy mercy. How then can I hope for mercy?

What must I do? I truly know that I deserve not to appear before Thee, or to lift up my eyes to Thee. But whither can I go? Where can I hide myself from Thee? To whom can I go but to Thee?

Thou, LORD, art my Father and the Father of Mercies. I have ceased to act as a child, but Thou hast not left off to treat me as a Father. I have done all that could lead to my destruction; but Thou hast still in Thee all that is needful for my salvation. Thou hast made me, and saved me, and kept me.

If Thou cast me away, who will receive me? If Thou forsake me, who will take me up? I can call upon none but Thee. From none but Thee can I find relief.

Father, I come to Thee; I throw myself at Thy feet; I smite upon my breast; I humbly beg Thy mercy. Acknowledge a strayed sheep, that returns to Thee. I am wounded; Thou canst heal me. I am hungry; Thou canst feed me. I am filthy; Thou canst wash me. Thou canst save the dying: Thou canst raise the dead. Thy mercy is greater than my guilt: Thy goodness exceeds my sinfulness. Thou canst pardon more sins than I can commit. I have sinned, but Thou canst save. GOD be merciful to me a sinner.

36.—PRAYERS OF PENITENCE.

O GOD! I kneel before Thee with contrite heart, most humbly confessing my evil nature and wicked life. My thoughts, words, and deeds have been full of sin, and my heart cries out against me. But Thou art greater than my heart, and knowest all that I have done.

O Searcher of hearts! Thou knowest how often I have vowed to serve Thee better, and how shamefully I have broken my vows. I have begun to seek Thy face; and have gone back to vanity, and lost myself in it.

With grief of heart and shame of face I confess that I have by word and example [and by —] led others to rebel against Thee; and have shared the guilt of their sins. Thou hast been and art to me a good and gracious GOD; but I have been unworthy and vile.

LORD, for Thy tender mercies' sake, let my sins, which are many, be forgiven me. And let Thy Holy Spirit teach and help me to live in purity and truth before Thee. Lighten my darkness by the brightness of Thy truth. Warm my heart with the fire of love. GOD, be merciful to me a sinner, for JESUS CHRIST'S sake. Amen.

O merciful GOD, Thou hast shewed great mercy to me, and hast done great things for me; but I have wandered away from Thee. I have often resolved and promised to amend my life, but have returned again to my evil way. I have sinned against the light of Thy gospel and Thy great love to me, against the terrors of Thy law, the rebukes of Thy Spirit, and the checks of my own conscience. LORD, if Thou wilt, Thou canst make me clean. Absolve me, I pray Thee, from the guilt of sin; save me from its punishment; cleanse me from its stain; free me from its power. Forgive my folly, and strengthen my weakness. Draw me by Thy grace here, and crown me with Thy glory hereafter; for the LORD JESUS CHRIST'S sake. Amen.

LORD JESUS, remember me, and lay not my sins to my charge; for truly I knew not what I did when I sinned. By Thy sweat and great drops of blood; Thy soul in agony; Thy weeping eyes; Thine ears filled with insults; Thy mouth moistened with vinegar and gall; Thy face shamefully defiled by spitting; Thy neck weighed down with the burden of the cross; Thy back furrowed with stripes and wounds; Thy pierced hands and feet; Thy strong cry, Eli, Eli; Thy heart pierced with the spear; Thy Body broken; Thy Blood shed;—LORD, forgive the offence of Thy servant, and cover all his sins. Shew me Thy mercy, O LORD; and grant me Thy salvation; now and evermore. Amen.

LORD, I believe that Thou didst create me: despise not the work of Thy hands—that Thou madest me after Thine image and likeness: suffer not Thy likeness to be blotted out—that Thou hast redeemed me with Thy Blood: suffer not the price of Thy redemption to be lost: that Thou hast called me a Christian after Thy Name: despise not Thine own title—that Thou hast sanctified me in regeneration: destroy not Thy holy work—that Thou hast grafted me into the good olive tree: cut not off a member of Thy body.

O think upon Thy servant as concerning Thy word, wherein Thou hast caused me to put my trust. My soul hath longed for Thy salvation, and I have a good hope because of Thy word. Amen.

LORD, I cast myself down before Thee: O cast me not away from Thee! I cannot stand at the bar of Thy justice, so I fall down at the footstool of Thy mercy. I condemn myself for my sins: LORD, enter not into judgment with me. Wash away my sins in my Saviour's Blood, and cleanse my soul in the streams of mercy. O GOD of all grace, I pray Thee so to pardon me a sinner as to number me with Thy saints. Give me strength to kill my lusts, and care to watch against and withstand all occasions and temptations to sin—especially against those that are by nature, custom, or condition of life most ready to surprise me. Teach me to watch and pray and strive; and let Thy Holy Spirit help and strengthen me, that I may gain the victory at last; for His sake who overcame the world for me, the Captain of my Salvation, Thy Dear Son, JESUS CHRIST my LORD. Amen.

[*See Chapters* 124, 125, 127.]

37.—SEVEN DEADLY SINS.

[*The Seven " Penitential" Psalms may be used with the Prayers.*]

Sunday.—PRIDE.—*Psalm* 32.

Morning.—Take from me, O LORD, the evil spirit of pride, and clothe me with humility. Grant that I may meekly bear the yoke of Him That humbled Himself to the death and shame of the Cross, and is now exalted in glory. Teach me to adore and copy the spirit which He hath set before us in His words and by His most holy example.

Evening.—LORD, keep me from the sin of pride. Let me never exalt myself before Thee or against Thee. Preserve in me an humble spirit; that Thou mayest approve me on earth, and at last exalt me to glory; for His sake Who so abased Himself because of my pride, JESUS CHRIST my Saviour. *Amen.*

Monday.—COVETOUSNESS.— Psalm 102.

Morning.—LORD, suffer not my heart to desire the things of this life. Teach me to be content with what Thy love qas given, and freely to give to others what I have freely received.

Evening.—LORD, Who art rich in mercy, give me on earth enough to bring me to Heaven, and let me covet nothing more. Let me rather suffer want here for a time, than hereafter for ever. Teach me so to enjoy and dispense what I have on earth, that I may receive it again from Thee in Heaven; for the sake of Him Who for my sake became poor, JESUS CHRIST my Saviour. *Amen.*

Tuesday.—LUST.—*Psalm* 51.

Morning.—Make me a clean heart, O GOD, and fill me with holy desires; that no thought of impurity may rest in my heart, no unclean word be spoken by my tongue, no unholy act defile the temple of the Holy Ghost.

Evening.—O GOD, Who art of purer eyes than to behold iniquity: Keep me from all filthiness of flesh and spirit; that before Thee, Who seest both, I may be without stain. And grant that, as I have been made a member of the pure Body of CHRIST, I may have the help of Thy Holy Spirit, in keeping under my evil desires, and in filling my heart with good desires; for the merits of Thy Holy One, JESUS CHRIST my Saviour. *Amen.*

Wednesday.—ANGER—*Psalm* 6.

Morning.—O Almighty Judge of men and angels, give me a meek and gentle spirit; that I may escape Thy anger, and may abide in Thy love.

Evening.—LORD, keep all angry passions out of my heart and mouth. Suffer me not to take into my hands the sword of vengeance, lest I fall justly by Thy sword. Though flesh and blood excite me, let Thy Holy Spirit restrain me; that I may be like

Thee, my Heavenly Father, in kindness and mercy; for the sake of the Lamb of GOD, JESUS CHRIST my Saviour. *Amen.*

Thursday.—GLUTTONY.— *Psalm* 38.

Morning.—LORD, give me grace to be moderate in food, to feed the hungry, to hunger and thirst after Thee and the good things that Thou hast prepared for them that love Thee.

Evening.—LORD, help me to be sober and temperate. Let me not lose my soul by abusing my body. Let my eating, and drinking, and all that I do, be to Thy glory. Let me not be driven from Paradise and its fruits by eating forbidden fruit in this world. Teach me to prepare for the good things that Thou hast provided in the Heavenly Feast, by following the example of Him Whose meat and drink it was to do Thy Will, JESUS CHRIST my Saviour. Amen.

Friday.—ENVY.—*Psalm* 130.

Morning.—O most gracious Father, help me to desire and to seek the good of my neighbour; and to rejoice in all good things which Thou doest or givest unto him.

Evening.—O LORD, let not mine eye be evil because Thou art good. Make me submit to Thy will, when I am in trouble, and make me rejoice at Thy acts of kindness, when my neighbour prospers. Teach me to love my enemies, for the sake of Him Who died for His enemies, JESUS CHRIST my Saviour. Amen.

Saturday.—SLOTH—*Psalm* 143.

Morning.—LORD, hear me when I pray, and help me to serve Thee with my body and my spirit. Make it my delight to do Thy will; I ask no rest from Thy service here below: when the work of this life is over, let me serve Thee in Thy temple above, with those who rest not day and night.

Evening.—O GOD, Who hast given to every man his own place and his own work: Keep me from the great evil of an idle life. Let me not spend my precious days in vain. Help me to labour for my soul more than my body; to do what good I can to all men and, above all things, to serve and fear Thee. Teach me to redeem what is lost of my time, and so to spend what is left that I may live for ever with thee in the world to come; through the merits of Him Whose life was a constant labour to do all good to every man, JESUS CHRIST my Saviour. Amen.

38.—HYMNS.

Come Thou weary wandering child,
  Far away from home;
Leave these deserts bleak and wild,
  Where the wretched roam.

Why so long do sinful chains
  Hold Thee in their thrall?
Why beneath thy heavy pains
  Dost thou faint and fall?

Why endure a mournful life,
  Lonely and unblest?
Why go on in toil and strife,
  Turning from Thy rest?

Hast thou never heard of One
  Who has loved Thee well?
Who, to bring Thee joy, has done
  More than words can tell.

I have all Thy sorrows borne,
  I have conquered sin:
Loved of JESUS, cease to mourn,
  Thou canst glory win.

Come with all Thy sin and care,
  Heavy though they be;
I the crushing load will bear,
  Lay it all on me.

Bring the shame that makes thee feel
  Ready to despair,
When the Spirit bids thee kneel
  To thy GOD in prayer.

Bring thy guilt, and pain, and woe,
  They shall all be mine;
In their place I will bestow
  Grace and joy divine.

Lay thy doubts and fears aside,
  Only trust in Me;
For thy sake I lived and died,
  Now I live for thee.

All the work that I have done
  Was to bring thee rest;
All the gifts My love has won
  Are to make thee blest.

Let me wash thee in the blood
  That for thee was shed;
Take from Me the Heavenly Food'—
  True and living bread.

Healed by Me, thy soul shall live
  In immortal health;
From my treasure I will give
  Never-failing wealth.

When the conflict deeper grows,
  In thy sorrow's night,
I will shield thee from thy foes,
  I will be thy light.

I will guide thee in the way
  With a gentle hand;
And will bring thee day by day
  Towards a brighter land.

Take the gifts my love supplies,
  And, when life is o'er,
Share with me beyond the skies
  Joy for evermore.
              T. B. P.

Loving Saviour hear me,
  On Thy Name I call;
Bring Thy mercy near me,
  Be my life, my All.

I had none to save me,
 Nothing of my own,
Till Thy promise gave me
 Hope in Thee alone.

I am lost without Thee;
 Sin's unhappy slave;
May I never doubt Thee,
 JESU, strong to save.

May I see Thee bleeding
 On the shameful tree,
And in heaven pleading
 What Thou didst for me.

All my past misdoing
 Teach me to confess
When for mercy suing,
 Give me lowliness.

See me humbly kneeling;
 Thou canst make me whole,
Bring Thy strength and healing
 To my weary soul.

Cleanse the evil staining
 Life, and thought, and heart;
Leave no spot remaining
 In my inmost part.

May I see Thee bending
 O'er me from above,
And the Spirit sending
 With Thy gifts of love.

May I bow before Thee
 With a holy fear,
And in love adore Thee
 As my Saviour dear.

In each sore temptation
 Turn my heart to Thee;
Be my strong salvation,
 Be my purity.

Be my strength in weakness,
 Be my peace in strife
Come, with Thine own meekness,
 Quieting my life.

When I faint in sorrow,
 Bring Thy comfort near;
When I dread the morrow,
 Come with hope to cheer.

Faithful Shepherd feed me
 In the pastures green,
Faithful Shepherd, lead me
 Where Thy steps are seen.

Hold me fast, and guide me
 In the narrow way,
So, with Thee beside me,
 I shall never stray.

Daily bring me nearer
 To the Heavenly shore;
May Thy love grow dearer,
 May I love Thee more.

Hallow every pleasure,
 Sanctify my pain,
Be Thyself my Treasure,
 Though none else I gain.

Give me joy or sadness;
 This be all my care,
That eternal gladness
 I with Thee may share.

Day by day prepare me,
 As Thou seest best,
Then let angels bear me
 To Thy promised rest.

When the world is failing
 From my mortal sight,
Lift the shadows veiling
 Worlds more pure and bright.

When the world for ever
 Is no more to me,

Bring me where I never
  Shall depart from Thee.

Oh! the joy of winning
  This reward at last;
All my dread of sinning,
  All my mourning past!

By Thy Cross and dying,
  Jesu, hear my prayer;
Daily grace supplying,
  Bring me safely there.
T. B. P.

How can I seek Thy Presence,
  O my God?
How can I hope that Thou
  wilt pardon me?
Thou knowest all the paths of
  sin I trod,
In my long wandering away
  from Thee.

How can I meet Thine eye,
  how can I dare
With my unworthy lips to
  speak Thy Name?
How can I hope Thy love
  again to share.
All covered as I am with
  guilt and shame?

I was Thy child, Thou madest
  me Thine own,
The holy sign was marked
  upon my brow;
By daily gifts Thy love to me
  was shewn;
Is there a hope that Thou
  dost love me now?

I am in want, I have spent
  all, and now,
Those wasted years can
  never more be mine:

My Father, I have learned
  that only Thou
Canst help me from Thy
  store of love divine.

Thou art my only hope: I
  have no claim
Upon Thy mercy; I am so
  defiled:
But I will dare to call Thee
  by Thy Name;
I am a prodigal, but still
  Thy child.

My Father, I have sinned, and
  now I lie
In bitter shame, and all my
  sin deplore;
I only long to serve Thee till
  I die,
And never leave Thee,
  never pain Thee more.

I know Thy love will follow
  to the last
Thy children who have wandered far away.
Thy love has taught me now
  to hate the past,
And in my shame it teaches
  me to pray.

My Father, for the sake of
  Him Who died—
Pardon me—wash me clean
  from guilty stain,
And let me never wander
  from Thy side,
Or fail in faithfulness and
  love again.
T. B. P.

Before the door of every heart
  Oppressed with sin and care,

A loving Saviour stands and knocks,
  Entreating entrance there.
So many days and nights have passed,
  So many years have gone,
And yet He patient lingers there,
  And gently knocketh on.

The frost has chilled those bleeding wounds,
  That tell us of His Love,—
All borne that we might dwell with Him
  In happy homes above.

How weary are those tender feet,
  How sad that loving face,
How numbed those hands that long to clasp
  Us in a fond embrace!

O heart of mine, and can'st thou bid
  Thy loving Saviour wait
Mid winter's cold and frost and snow,
  Still knocking at thy gate?

O open wide the door to Him,
  A lodging sweet prepare;
When others drive Him from their hearts,
  Let Him find refuge there.

O joy of joys, O Heaven on earth
  When Jesus fills the heart,
O happiness that knows no bounds,
  O bliss that knows no smart!

A. J. B.

Holy Jesu! I have crowned Thee
  With a crown of piercing thorn,
And have stood with those around Thee,
  Who have loaded Thee with scorn.

Oh! how oft with sin I've scourged Thee.
  Buffeted Thy sacred face!
Up dark Calvary's hill I've urged Thee
  To Thy death of deep disgrace.

I have nailed Thee, faint and bleeding,
  To the tree, the shameful tree,
All Thy pangs and woes unheeding,
  Pitying not Thy misery.

I have made the blood flow streaming
  From Thy sacred hands and feet;
Not one act of love redeeming
  All my cruelty complete.

Jesu! grant me true contrition
  For these bitter sins of mine;
Tears that know no intermission,
  Penitence, and grace divine.

Give me, Lord, Thine absolution
  From the sins I now abhor,
And the stedfast resolution
  Never to offend Thee more,

By Thy Cross, Thy bitter Passion,
By Thy suff'rings all for me,
By Thy great, Thy sweet compassion,
Hear, O LORD, my Litany.
A. J. B.

Saviour most loving, bending before Thee,
Sinful and mourning, Thy mercy we crave;
Leave us not hopeless, LORD we implore Thee,
Thou hast redeemed us, O hear and save.

Fountain, where sinners find ever flowing
Streams that wash all their defilement away;
To those pure waters thankfully going,
We would for mercy and cleansing pray.

Gentle physician, mortal ills healing,
Bending in love o'er each sin-stricken soul;
Come, all Thy care and goodness revealing,
Strengthen our weakness and make us whole.

Shepherd most careful, warn us when straying,
Guide us in paths where Thine own feet have trod;
Led by Thy call, Thy dear voice obeying,
Bring us in peace to the fold of GOD.

Light where the path is shadowed and dreary,
Friend of the hearts that in loneliness pine;
Help of the poor, and strength of the weary,
Where is the love that is like to Thine!

LORD, Thou dost love us, for Thy love sought us
When we were wandering in deserts alone;
LORD, Thou dost love us, for Thy blood bought us,
And Thou wilt never forget Thine own.

LORD, we would trust Thee, doubting Thee never;
Help us in faith on Thy Word to recline:
LORD, we would love Thee; keep us for ever
Near to that tenderest heart of Thine.

LORD, we would follow where Thou dost call us,
Patient in sorrow and valiant in fight;
May we be true whatever befall us,
Journeying on to the land of light.

There, LORD, with gladness laying before Thee
Each heavy cross we have carried so long;
Crowned with Thy blessing we shall adore Thee,
Singing for ever the triumph song.
T. B. P.

PART III.—HOLY COMMUNION.

"Arise, O LORD GOD, into Thy Resting-place."—*2 Chronicles* vi. 41.

39.—GOING TO CHURCH.

Many people think that they need not go to Church. They sit at home, and perhaps read a little in their Bibles. This, they tell us, is all that GOD asks from them.

This is a great sin. For, you know, we are not saved by going straight to GOD the Father. JESUS CHRIST says, "No man cometh unto the Father, but by Me." We must come to JESUS, or we need not try to come at all. And JESUS has told us how to come to Him. We "must be born again" of water and of the Spirit. It is only as members of His Church that the LORD JESUS CHRIST receives us. When we are baptized into the Church of CHRIST, then CHRIST owns us as His people. It is very plain that we must act like members of CHRIST's Church, or we lose the blessings we have got by being born into it. Even though there were no special blessings to be got at Church, we would lose our place in the Church of CHRIST, if we never came to claim it. Keep in mind those words of GOD—"Not forsaking the assembling of ourselves together, as the manner of some is." *Heb.* x. 25. Is that *your* manner?

Church Services.

You will find the Services of the Church in your Prayer Book. Morning Prayer or Mattins, Litany, and Evening Prayer or Evensong, are the chief services that are in constant use. Most of the Prayers and portions of Holy Scripture in them have been in the Church Services for many hundred years. It is a very good thing for you to go to Church and join in the prayers, as often as you can—and that not on Sundays only, but on week-days too. Take care to join in the service with your heart and your lips. [*Prayers before and after Service, p.* 80.]

Divine Service.

Only one of the Services used at Church has GOD as its author, and is in this sense Divine. The Sacrament of the Altar was ordained by the LORD JESUS CHRIST Himself. He did not appoint any other Service. He gave us one

D

Prayer—the LORD's Prayer—and told us, "when we pray," to use it. So, as He also gave us one Service, we may be sure that "when" we meet in Church to worship GOD, we must put that Service in the highest place. 1 Cor. xi. 18, 20.

The Divine Service has many names:—

1. The Sacrament of the Altar; because of the *place* where It is celebrated. *Heb.* xiii. 10.

2. The Sacrament of the Body and Blood of CHRIST; because of the *Presence* of our Saviour's Body and Blood on the Altar in this Service. 1 Cor. xi. 27.

3. The Eucharist; because it is an offering of *thanks* and praise to GOD. This word is applied to the service in the Bible. 1 Cor. xiv. 16. 1 S. Tim. ii. 1.

4. The Mass; either because of the words with which the people are in some countries *sent* away at the end of the service, or because It is the Christian *Sacrifice*. This word is in such names as Christmas, Candlemas, and Lammas. 1 Cor. xi. 26.

5. The LORD's Supper; because in It we *eat* the Flesh of CHRIST, and *drink* His Blood.

6. The Holy Communion; because in it we are *made one* with CHRIST, and CHRIST with us. 1 Cor. x. 16.

7. The Liturgy; because it is the *Service* that GOD gave, and in which His Priests minister. *Acts* xiii. 2.

It is offered chiefly for four ends:—

1. For the honour and glory of GOD.

2. As an offering of thanks and praise to GOD for what He gives us.

3. For getting pardon of sin from GOD.

4. For seeking help and blessing through JESUS CHRIST.

You *ought* to attend the Church Services often: you *must*, if be a Christian, attend the Divine Service as often as you can. You cannot put any ordinance of man above the ordinance of GOD, which He appointed for constant use in His Church. Don't put the Church above the Saviour: if you do this, you sin very much, and must pray for pardon. You must not choose the service you like best, or go to Church at the time that is most convenient. Your duty is to ask when the Divine Service is used and to attend It. After you have done this, you may go to the Church Services, if you can.

40.—THE REAL PRESENCE.

All the names given by the Church to the Divine Service, and mentioned in the last chapter, may be used by Christian people. Indeed, the best way is to keep them all in mind; for each of them tells us something about the doctrine of the Service. They do not teach us different doctrines, but different parts of the same doctrine. There is one great doctrine of this Sacrament which is taught us, more or less, by all the seven names. That doctrine is the truth of the Real Presence of the LORD JESUS in the Sacrament. Let me show you how needful it it is to hold this truth firmly.

It is the Presence of our Saviour on earth that saves us—" CHRIST JESUS *came* into the world to save sinners." 1 *S. Tim.* i. 15. It is true, for GOD tells us, that JESUS CHRIST was made man—that He was an infant, a child, a youth, a man of sorrows. But we ask, Is JESUS present with us now? He is gone into Heaven, and will come again. In the meantime is He present or absent?

The LORD Himself has told us the truth. You will find what He says about it in *S. Matt.* xxvi. 26-28; *S. Mark* xiv. 22-24; *S. Luke* xxii. 19, 20; and 1 *Cor.* xi. 23-25. JESUS took bread and blessed it, and brake it, and said of it, THIS IS MY BODY. He took wine and blessed it, and said of it, THIS IS MY BLOOD. We must take these precious words just as they stand, and try to believe them.

It will not be hard for us to believe what GOD says, if we think of His power and His goodness. He Who gave His Son to die for us can give Him to be our Food. GOD fed His people in the wilderness with bread from heaven, *Exod.* xiv. 4; and JESUS says that He is "the true bread from heaven." *S. John* vi. 32. The LORD's Prayer teaches us to pray for daily bread; and the LORD says, "The bread that I will give is My Flesh, which I will give for the life of the world." *S. John* vi. 51. Even the devil believed that JESUS could turn stones into bread; and Christian people cannot doubt that He can give His Body under the form of bread. JESUS, Who changed water into wine —*S. John* ii.—can give His Blood under the form of wine. We must not wait for our eyes to tell us that JESUS is present; for "we walk by faith, not by sight." 2 *Cor.* v. 7. And if we ask how we are to walk by faith in this case, we learn from S. Paul that "faith cometh by hearing, and hearing by the word of GOD." *Rom.* x. 17. It is no matter what we see: we are to believe what we hear; and JESUS, the Word of GOD, says of the Bread and Wine—THIS IS MY BODY— THIS IS MY BLOOD.

D 2

There are two things about the Real Presence that we must be sure to believe:—

1. It is the LORD JESUS CHRIST Himself that comes to us in the Sacrament of the Altar. He comes to us in His two natures, both GOD and Man. For you know that our Blessed Saviour has not cast off His Human Body, but is still and for ever both GOD and Man—GOD as He was from the beginning in His glory—Man with His glorified Body. JESUS, the Son of GOD, came once from heaven and was made man; JESUS, the Son of Man, went up to heaven; JESUS, God and Man, comes down now to the altars of His Church.

2. The LORD JESUS is really present in the Sacrament of the Altar. It is not that you think He is present with you, or feel that Divine Presence. It is not fancy, but truth. As JESUS once "came unto His own, and His own received Him not,"—*S. John* i. 11,— so He comes now to the worthy and the unworthy. JESUS was Present to "the disciple whom JESUS loved" and to "the traitor." Our faith does not make JESUS Present: our unbelief does not make JESUS Absent. Man is nothing and can do nothing. GOD is the only worker. GOD only can make GOD Present anywhere. Nothing but the mighty words of JESUS, spoken by His Priests in the Consecration Prayer, can "bring CHRIST down from above." *Rom.* x. 6. It is not, then, a matter of feeling or of fancy. We do not feel GOD's influence in the Blessed Sacrament. We do not make Him Present by our faith. We believe that He *is* Present.

41.—SACRIFICE.

There is only one true and perfect Sacrifice—the offering of our LORD JESUS CHRIST on the Cross to take away our sins. The sacrifices under the Law only showed forth that one sacrifice, till JESUS came. Now, in the Sacrament of the Altar we "shew the LORD's death till He come" again. 1 *Cor.* xi. 26.

Our Christian Sacrifice is not like the Jewish sacrifices. Under the Law "the blood of bulls and goats" was offered; but now we have the offering of "the Precious Blood of CHRIST, as of a Lamb, without blemish and without spot." 1 *S. Peter* i. 19. For JESUS said, "The bread that I will give is My Flesh;" and gives us, at the Altar, His Body, "broken" and His Blood "shed."

When you think of the Christian Sacrifice, keep these two things in mind:—

1. There is only one High Priest. The Jewish Priest-

hood is gone. The LORD JESUS CHRIST is our great High Priest, after the order of Melchisedeck. He brings forth Bread and Wine for us. *Heb.* iv. 14, v. 10; *Gen.* xiv. 18. The Priests, that He has sent out, do nothing of themselves. They only do what the High Priest told them. *S. Luke* xxii. 19.

2. There is only one Sacrifice. All the Jewish sacrifices are gone. The LORD JESUS CHRIST offered one Sacrifice on the Cross, and there can be no other. Besides, that one sacrifice can never be repeated. It can only be pleaded and applied in the way GOD appoints.

In one way the LORD JESUS offered Himself to GOD all His life on earth; in another way, when He "brought forth Bread and Wine;" in another way, when He was crucified. This one offering is now applied in two ways— JESUS pleads His sacrifice for us *in Heaven*, by "appearing in the presence of GOD for us," *Heb.* ix. 24; JESUS pleads His sacrifice for us *on earth*, when He "appears" on the altars of His Church.

You see, then, what the Christian Sacrifice means. JESUS is our one High Priest: *therefore* He has Priests to serve under Him on earth. The one Sacrifice of the Cross is perfect: *therefore* it is pleaded continually in Heaven and earth to save our souls.

"We have an *altar*" for sacrifice, and are "partakers of the LORD's *table*." *Heb.* xiii. 10; 1 *Cor.* x. 21. Either word will do. All Christians are sacrificing priests; for they join in the sacrifice which the appointed priests offer in the Name of the High Priest. 1 *S. Peter* ii. 5; 1 *Cor.* x. 16.

42.—COMPANION TO THE ALTAR.

Communion in the Prayers.

The last three Chapters set before you what you must do to get the benefits of the Sacrament of the Altar.

1. It is, you see. the Divine Service; that is, it is appointed by GOD. So you *must* attend this service.

2. The LORD JESUS CHRIST is present in It; so you must "come before His Presence" as *often* as you can. *Ps.* xcv. 2.

3. It is the Christian Sacrifice—the Service by which we join on earth in the work of CHRIST in Heaven, and plead for all the benefits of our Saviour's death. So you must *with all your heart* join in the service when you come to it.

For all these reasons Christians take delight in decorating the Altar with its ornaments, and doing all they can to show their faith and love. JESUS lay in a manger once: let Him have a throne now.

Even if you have not yet received the Holy Communion, you may attend the service and have Communion in the Prayers. Don't give up the smaller blessing because you cannot yet claim the greater. You cannot learn to come to JESUS by staying away from Him. As a baptized Christian you have a right to attend this service. Use what you have well, and GOD will give you more: "He that hath, to him shall be given." *S. Mark* iv. 25.

The Communion Service.

The LORD's Service begins with the LORD's Prayer and a short Collect. Then the Priest reads the Ten Commandments; the people nine times pray for mercy and grace, and after the Tenth Commandment, beseech GOD to write all His laws in their hearts. The Collect for the Church and Queen comes next. Then you turn to the Collect for the Day. After it the Epistle is read. The Holy Gospel, which comes next, has in it some of our Saviour's words or tells us of Him, so all stand up when it is read. In the Creed we have the faith of the Gospel in the words of the Church; and in the Sermon, when there is one, we have some teaching on the Gospel, or the Creed, or some other part of the truth from one of GOD's ministers. Before the Sermon notices are given out, and the people are told of the Feasts and Fasts.

After the Sermon the people make offerings to GOD of money—"They shall not appear before the LORD empty." *Deut.* xvi. 16. All Christians should offer what they can to GOD. But, if you have no money, you can join equally with other people in the greater offering. The money is given to GOD on the Altar; but the offering that GOD requires is the Bread and Wine, which are, at this part of the Service, presented on the Altar by the Priest, as the Church orders. The Prayer for the Church is then read. In it we ask GOD to accept our alms and offerings, that is, the money and the Bread and Wine. Then, in the same prayer, we ask blessings for all set over GOD's people in the Church and State, and for all the people of GOD.

You will find that three long exhortations follow here. The first of them will help you to prepare for receiving the Communion; the second shows you the great need of receiving It; and the third the great danger of coming unprepared. These exhortations are sometimes used during the Service. Then follows a short exhortation beginning with the words—"Ye that do truly." It tells us, in few words, what we ought to be when we come to receive the Blessed Sacrament. Next come the Confession, Absolution, and some words of comfort from the Bible. Then, in preparation for the solemn part of the Service which is to follow, the Priest says to the people, "Lift up your hearts." After this, we find the "Preface," so called because it is an offering of praise that *comes before* the Consecration. At the end of the Preface comes the angels' song spoken of in the Preface. All the people begin to join in this at the words "Holy, Holy, Holy." The prayer "We do not presume," like the Confession and other parts of the Service, may be joined in by all who, at the time, are about to receive the Communion, or intend soon to prepare themselves for It.

All that has been said so far is only the preparation for that which is indeed the Divine Service — I mean the CONSECRATION, in which the Priest speaks the words and performs the acts given by our Saviour Himself. When the prayer is said, bow down humbly and worship the LORD—"seeing Him Who is invisible." During the Communion of the Priest and of the people, there is time for adoration and prayer. Do not lose these few precious minutes. Worship the LORD JESUS, Who comes to hear you and to bless you. "Let your requests be made known unto GOD."

When the Priest begins the LORD's Prayer say it after him, praying earnestly for the "daily bread" which the LORD gives to His people. Then in the Prayer that follows make an offering of yourself, with all you have and are, in union with the offering of CHRIST. The angels' hymn, "Glory be to GOD on high," teaches you again to adore your Saviour with all your heart. Then with the blessing of GOD's peace you may go to your home with gladness and thankfulness. Do not go away from Church, or even rise from your knees, till the Priest has left the altar. Think of the Service in which you have joined. Thank GOD for all his benefits. Ask Him to forgive the defects of your prayers, and to accept them for JESUS CHRIST's sake.

Devotions.

[*All the Prayers in this Chapter may be used when you are present at the Sacrament of the Altar, whether you receive the Holy Communion or not. Also the Hymns in Chapter 43.*]

When you kneel down.

In the Name of the ✠ Father, and of the Son, and of the Holy Ghost. Amen.

Take away from us, O LORD, we beseech Thee, all our sins, that we may be able to enter with pure hearts into the Holy of Holies.

O merciful LORD, incline Thine ears to our prayers, and enlighten our souls by the grace of Thy Holy Spirit, that we may worthily celebrate Thy Holy Mysteries, and love Thee with an everlasting love.

O GOD, Who in this wonderful Sacrament hast left unto us a Memorial of Thy Passion: Grant to us, we beseech Thee, so to venerate the Sacred Mysteries of Thy Body and Blood that we may always feel in ourselves the fruit of Thy Redemption; Who livest and reignest with the Father and the Holy Ghost, One GOD, world without end. men.

Forth from the dark and stormy sky,
LORD, to Thine Altar's shade we fly:
Forth from the world, its hope and fear,
Saviour, we seek Thy shelter here:
Weary and weak, Thy grace we pray;
Turn not, O LORD, Thy guests away.

When you offer your alms.

Blessed be Thou, O LORD GOD; for all things come of Thee, and of Thine own do we give Thee.

While the Bread and Wine are offered on the Altar.

In the spirit of humility and with contrite hearts may we be accepted of Thee, O LORD; and may our offering be so made in Thy sight, that it may be accepted of Thee, and may please Thee, O LORD our GOD.

Wash me, LORD JESUS, in Thy Precious Blood, that I may stand before Thee in truth and purity all my days.

Before the Consecration.

Most merciful GOD, look graciously upon the gifts now lying before Thee, and send down Thy Holy Spirit upon this Sacrifice; that he may make this Bread the Body of Thy CHRIST, and this Cup the Blood of Thy CHRIST.

Blessed is He that cometh in the Name of the LORD. Hosanna in the highest.

After the Consecration.

It is the LORD! LORD I believe: help Thou mine unbelief. LORD JESUS! have mercy upon me.

Hail Saving Victim, offered for me and all mankind on the Cross! Hail Precious Blood, flowing from the side of my LORD JESUS CHRIST, and washing away the stains of all sins, new and old! Cleanse, sanctify, and keep my soul unto everlasting life. Amen.

LORD, receive this sacrifice, which is offered as a memorial of our Saviour's Passion, Resurrection, and Ascension. Grant that we may die with Him to our sins, rise with Him to a new life, and ascend with Him to Thee.

Worthy is the Lamb that was slain. Blessing, and honour, and glory, and power, be unto Him that sitteth upon the throne and unto the Lamb for ever and ever.

Help me to adore Thee, Saviour, GOD Unseen,
Veiling now Thy glory under shadows mean.
Low before Thy Presence all my soul is bowed,
As by faith I see Thee shrin'd within the cloud.
Shepherd of the faithful, saying "It is I,"
Bid my faith more simply on Thy word rely.

LORD JESUS, I adore Thee present in this Holy Sacrament. I believe that Thou art here. All my hope is in Thee. I desire to love Thee with my whole heart. Come to me, and help me. Feed me, for I am hungry. Strengthen me, for I am weak. Heal me, for I am sick. Give me life, that I may never die. Save me from all my sins. Teach me to obey Thy Commandments. O let me be Thine, and do Thou, O my Saviour, be mine from henceforth and for ever. Grant that nothing in life or death may ever separate me from Thee any more. In this one prayer hear me, O LORD; and in all things else do with me as Thou wilt.

O Lamb of GOD, that takest away the sins of the world, have mercy upon us.

O Lamb of GOD, that takest away the sins of the world, have mercy upon us.

O Lamb of GOD, that takest away the sins of the world, grant us Thy peace.

O Saving Victim, opening wide
The gate of heaven to man below;
Our foes press on from every side:
Thine Aid supply, Thy Strength bestow.

We pray Thee, help Thy servants, whom Thou hast redeemed with Thy Precious Blood. Make them to be numbered with Thy saints in glory everlasting.

We commend unto Thy mercy, O LORD, all Thy servants, who are gone before us with the sign of faith, and now rest in the sleep of peace; especially—Grant unto them, we beseech Thee, a place of

refreshment, light, and peace.
Our Father [*Say the Lord's Prayer.*]

43.—HYMNS.

All hail Redeemer of mankind!
Thy life on Calvary resigned
  Did fully once for all atone;
Thy Blood hath paid our utmost price,
Thine all-sufficient Sacrifice
  Remains eternally alone.

Angels and men might strive in vain,
They could not add the smallest grain
  T' augment Thy death's atoning power;
Thy Sacrifice is all complete,
The death Thou never canst repeat,
  Once offered up to die no more.

Yet may we celebrate below,
And daily thus Thine Offering show
  Exposed before Thy Father's eyes!
In this Tremendous Mystery
Present Thee bleeding on the Tree
  Our Everlasting Sacrifice.

By the picture of Thy Passion
  Still in pain I remain
Waiting for salvation.

Jesu, let Thy sufferings ease me;
Saviour, Lord, speak the word,
By Thy death release me.

At Thy Cross behold me lying;
  Make my soul throughly whole
By Thy Blood's applying.

Hear me, Lord, my sins confessing;
  Now relieve, Saviour give;—
Give me now Thy Blessing.

Still my cruel sins oppress me;
  Tied and bound, till the sound
Of Thy voice release me.

Call me out of condemnation;
  To my grave come and save;
Save me by Thy Passion.

To Thy foul and helpless creature
  Come and cleanse all my sins;
Come and change my nature.

Save me now and still deliver;
  Enter in, cast out sin,
Keep Thine house for ever.

With all the powers my poor soul hath,
Of humble love and loyal faith
Thus low, my God! I bow to Thee,
Whom so much love bow'd low for me.

Be still, vain thoughts of How and Why,
And all adore faith's mystery:

Faith is my skill, faith can believe
As fast as Love new laws can give.

Faith is my eye, faith strength affords
To keep pace with those powerful words:
And words more sure, more sweet than they,
Love could not think, Truth could not say.

O dear Memorial of that death,
Which still survives, and gives us breath!
Live ever, Bread of Life, and be
My food, my joy, my all to me.

Come, glorious LORD! my hopes increase,
And fill my portion in Thy peace:
Come, hidden life; and that long day
For which I languish, come away:

When this dry soul those eyes shall see,
And drink the unsealed source of Thee!
When glory's sun faith's shade shall chase,
And for Thy veil give me Thy face.

———

JESUS treads the floor of Heaven,
  JESUS reigns the angels' king:
JESUS is the Lamb they worship,
  JESUS is the Name they sing.
All His pain and woe are over,
  All the shame and bitterness;
Henceforth He in glory reigneth,
  King of might and righteousness.

Though our eyes no longer see Him,
  Still for us He intercedes,
And His Sacrifice prevailing
  Ever with the Father pleads.
And He longs to bring us all to
  That dear land of peace and love,
Ever, ever to be with Him
  In His palace bright above.

Angels there are gathered round Him
  In their nine-fold choirs they stand;
He the light, the joy, the beauty
  Of their ever-glorious band.
Gabriel is among their number
  Who the glorious message brought
Of the Saviour's Incarnation
  When that miracle was wrought.

There are angels who at Christmas
  Filled the air with sweetest song;

Singing still their hymn of
glory,
   As they round about Him
   throng:
And the one amazed who
witnessed
   That dread hour of agony,
When the blood-sweat poured
from Him,
   Prostrate in Gethsemane.

Those too who, at dawn of
Easter,
   Rolled the heavy stone
   away,
As He rose, o'er death triumphant,
   On the first bright Easter
   Day,
Stand around Him with bright-clad ones,
   Who to men of Galilee,
Spake and said, "as He had
left them,
   So His coming back should
   be."

O for faith to pierce the veil
that
   Hides Him from our longing eyes,
O for angels' wings to mount
up
   Far above the starry
   skies;
There to see Him in His
glory,
   There to worship at His
   Feet,
There to sing the song of
triumph
   There to know true bliss
   complete.

Patience, patience, soon the
summons
   To that holy land shall
   come,
And our weary wandering
footsteps
   Never more shall leave
   their home.
Jesus in Thy mercy grant us
   Strength to conquer in the
   strife,
Then hereafter we shall hymn
Thee
   In those blissful realms of
   life.   A. J. B.

44.—SPIRITUAL COMMUNION.

You can make an Act of Spiritual Communion at any time, either at Church or at home, when you do *not* receive the Holy Communion. When you attend the Sacrament of the Altar, you may use this devotion instead of some of those "After the Consecration," which are given in the last Chapter:—

Lord, I am not worthy that Thou shouldest come under my roof; but speak the word only, and my soul shall be healed.

Lord Jesus, I believe that Thou art truly present in the Most Holy Sacrament. I adore Thee; I am sorry that I have offended Thee, I love Thee. Come to my soul . . . ✝ . . . and never, never leave me.

Soul of Christ, sanctify me.
Body of Christ, save me.

Blood of CHRIST, gladden me.
Water out of the side of CHRIST, wash me.
Passion of CHRIST, strengthen me.
O good JESUS, hear me.
Hide me within Thy wounds.
Suffer me not to be separated from Thee.
From the malicious enemy defend me;
At the hour of my death call me,
And bid me come unto Thee
That, with Thy Saints, I may praise Thee
For ever and ever. Amen.

45.—GOING TO COMMUNION.

If you attend Church often, and join in the Prayers of the Communion Service, you will desire also to receive the Holy Communion. Perhaps you have felt this longing, but have never yet dared to come to the altar. What keeps you away? Examine yourself and see what the reason is. *Nothing* ought to keep you away. For instance—

1. You are not fit to come to Communion. If you mean by this that you are living in sin, then you are not fit. But, remember this, you are not fit to die.

2. You are not good enough. If you mean that you are trying to be good, and find it hard to keep from sin, then you ought to come. The blessing of Communion is for "the strengthening and refreshing" of weak and sorrowful souls like yours. [*See Church Catechism.*]

3. You don't know enough. But you are not asked to know a great deal. You are only asked to believe GOD's truth. If you have faith, you will very soon learn all that is needed.

4. You have too many cares. For this very reason you should come to Communion. The more the world drags you down, the more you need GOD's help against it.

5. Some people go to Communion, and get no good by it. If they come unworthily, let this warn you to come worthily, and prepare yourself for receiving so great a blessing.

6. Your neighbours will scoff at you. Don't mind this. Pray for them and for yourself. It is better that your neighbours should laugh at you, than that GOD should mourn over you. The LORD JESUS asks you to confess Him before men. Take up your cross, and follow Him.

7. You are afraid of falling back after Communion. You ought to fear this. But you ought also to fear keeping back now. Besides, you will get help from GOD, if you seek it; and, if you do GOD's will in this one thing, He will hear your prayers, when you

ask Him to help you in other duties.

8. The Communion is a very solemn thing. Yet, it is; for the LORD JESUS, your *Saviour*, is present in it. But you will have to stand before Him some day as your *Judge*. He is now your Saviour, as kind and good as ever He was when He walked on earth; and He says "Come unto Me."

Believe it, there is danger in coming unworthily; but there is also danger in staying away unworthily. JESUS CHRIST has said, "Except ye eat the flesh of the Son of Man, and drink His blood, ye have no life in you." *S. John* vi. 53.

46.—HOW TO GO TO COMMUNION.

Do not go to Communion without preparation. Ask your clergyman to help you. Be very careful about your First Communion. Think of the great blessing you seek. "Prepare to meet thy GOD."

You perhaps think that you are too young to be a communicant. You are not too young, if you are old enough to sin, to repent of sin, and to desire help to keep from sin.

You should receive the Holy Communion, if possible, at an early service, and before you have taken any food.

Devotions before Communion.

In the Name of the ✠ Father, and of the Son, and of the Holy Ghost. Amen.

Our Father. I believe.

Help me, LORD, to call my own ways to remembrance, and seriously think of the errors of the past; that I may enjoy the benefits of the Holy Sacrament and the blessings of the Heavenly Feast. [*See Instructions and Devotions, Part II.*]

Let Thy Holy Spirit so assist me, O most gracious Father, that my preparation for the Blessed Sacrament may be earnest and devout. Let nothing take away my heart from Thee, or change my resolves. Let me so eat the Flesh of CHRIST and drink His Blood; that, when I go hence, I may be admitted to the Marriage Supper of the Lamb; through the same JESUS CHRIST our LORD. Amen.

[*Add one or more of these Psalms*—63, 65, 84, 85, 86.]

During the Service you may use some of the Devotions given in Chapter 42. Before you go to the Altar say—LORD JESUS I adore Thee; I believe that Thou art present in this Sacrament; I hope in Thee; I love Thee; I desire to receive Thee, that I may feed on Thee, and never be separated from Thee.

At the Altar say—LORD, I am not worthy that Thou shouldest come under my roof;

but speak the word only, and my soul shall be healed.

When the Priest comes to you with the paten, open both your hands, and lay the right hand on the left in the form of a cross. After the words of the Priest, say—"Amen." When the Priest comes to you with the chalice, drink a few drops, saying "Amen" as before.

Go back to your place after a few moments, and kneel in silent adoration.

After Communion.

Thanks be unto GOD for His unspeakable gift. O LORD, whom have I in heaven but Thee, and there is none upon earth that I desire in comparison of Thee.

Soul of CHRIST. Chapter 44.

Truest Bread, Good Shepherd, tend us,
JESU, pity and befriend us;
Feed our souls, from ill defend us,
Sight of all Thy Goodness send us,
In the Land of Life and Light.
Thou Who all things canst and knowest,
Who on earth such Food bestowest,
Us, with Thy blest Saints, though lowest,
Where the Heavenly Feast Thou shewest,
Evermore in bliss unite.
Amen.

[*Add Prayers from Chapter* 42 *if you have time.*]

Grant, blessed GOD, that we and all Thy servants, who have received this Holy Communion may partake of all Its benefits. May we be so saved from the wiles of Satan, and so confirmed in the ways of godliness; that, being filled with Thy Holy Spirit, we may in this life be made worthy members of CHRIST's Body, and at last become heirs of eternal life; through the merits and mediation of JESUS CHRIST our Saviour. Amen.

Almighty GOD, Who hast united all Christians in one Brotherhood by the Holy Sacrament of the Altar: Let me be partaker of the prayers of all that this day receive the Holy Communion in all parts of the world; and let my prayers for them be accepted by Thee; for JESUS CHRIST's sake. Amen.

JESU, the true Paschal Food, By Thyself on Thine bestowed;
Miracle of mightiest love!
Living Bread of Heaven support me,
So no earthly chance may hurt me,
World, nor Flesh, nor Satan more.

Praised be the LORD for evermore. Amen and Amen.

47.—BEFORE AND AFTER PRAYER.

Before Private Prayer.

Unto Thee lift I up mine eyes, O Thou that dwellest in the heavens. Unto Thee, O LORD, will I lift up my soul.

Breathe on me, O GOD, by Thy Holy Spirit, that the breath of my spirit may now please Thee; and that my prayers may come up as sweet odours before Thee; through JESUS CHRIST my Saviour.

O LORD, open Thou my lips that I may bless Thy Holy Name; cleanse my heart from all vain, evil, and distracting thoughts; enlighten my understanding and purify my will; that I may perform this service with attention and devotion; and that my prayers and praises may be heard in the Presence of Thy glory. Amen.

After Private Prayer.

Pardon, O merciful GOD, all the defects of my prayers; grant all that I have prayed for, and all that I ought to have prayed for; and give me a share in all the blessings granted unto the devotions of Thy Holy Church; for JESUS CHRIST's sake. Amen.

Before Service at Church.

As for me, I will come into Thy House, even upon the multitude of Thy mercy, and in Thy fear will I worship toward Thy Holy Temple.

O LORD, hear the voice of my humble petitions, when I cry unto Thee; when I hold up my hands toward the mercy-seat of Thy Holy Temple.

We wait for Thy loving kindness, O GOD, in the midst of Thy Temple.

LORD, save me from wandering thoughts and looks, but chiefly from fixed lusts and habits of sin.

LORD, cleanse my heart and my lips, that I may be able to love and serve Thee as I ought; for JESUS CHRIST's sake. Amen.

After Service at Church.

LORD, hear my prayers, accept my praises, pardon my sins, teach me to do Thy will, and give me Thy blessing; for JESUS CHRIST's sake. Amen.

My soul, wait thou still upon GOD: for my hope is in Him. Amen.

PART IV.—ALL THE DAY LONG.

"They rest not day and night, saying Holy, Holy, Holy, Lord God Almighty."—*Revelations* iv. 8.

48.—THE MORNING.

Pray without ceasing.

The first thing in the morning light,
The chief thing through the busy day,
The last thing ere you sleep at night,
Should be to watch, and think, and pray.

Ejaculations.

Waking. When I wake up I am present with Thee.
Rising. ✢ Glory be to God Most High.
Washing. Make me a clean heart, O God.
Dressing. Clothe me, O Lord, with Thy grace.

Thoughts.

Open thine eyes, my soul, and see,
Once more the light returns to thee;
Look round about, and choose the way,
Thou mean'st to travel o'er to-day.

Think on the dangers thou may'st meet,
And always watch thy sliding feet;
Think where thou once hast fallen before;
And mark the place, and fall no more.

Think on the helps thy God bestows,
And cast to steer thy life by those;
Think on the sweets thy soul did fill,
When thou didst well, and do so still.

Think on the pains that shall torment
Those stubborn souls that ne'er repent;
Think on those joys that wait above,
To crown the head of holy love.

Think what at last will be thy part,
If thou goest on where now thou art;
See life and death set thee to choose,
One thou must take and one refuse.

O my dear Lord, guide Thou my course,

And draw me on with Thy sweet force;
Still make me walk, still make me tend,
By Thee my Way to Thee my End.

All glory to the Sacred Three, One Undivided Trinity;
As it hath been in ages gone, May now and ever still be done.
Amen.

Resolutions.

Confess fault's guilt,
  Crave pardon for thy sin;
Tread holy paths,
  Call grace to guide therein.

I will set GOD always before my face; I will take no wicked thing in hand; I will not go in the way of sinners; I will try not to——; I will try to ——. LORD, be Thou my helper.

Hymn.

Forth in Thy Name, O LORD, I go
  My daily labour to pursue:
Thee, only Thee, resolved to know,
  In all I think, or speak, or do.

The task Thy wisdom has assigned
  O let me cheerfully fulfil;
In all my works Thy Presence find,
  And prove Thine acceptable will

Preserve me from my calling's snare,
  And hide my simple heart above—
Above the thorns of choking care,
  The gilded baits of worldly love.

Thee may I set at my right hand,
  Whose eyes mine inmost substance see;
And labour on at Thy command,
  And offer all my works to Thee.

Give me to bear Thy easy yoke,
  And every moment watch and pray;
And still to things eternal look,
  And hasten to Thy glorious day:

For Thee delightfully employ
  Whate'er Thy bounteous grace hath given;
And run my course with even joy,
  And closely walk with Thee to heaven.
Amen.

Five Parts of Morning Prayer.

1. Be grateful.
2. Offer up thine heart.
3. Design thy daily task.
4. Shun sin.
5. Seek aid Divine.

49.—THE DAY.

Subjects for Meditation.

Go forth, my soul, another day,
Go forth upon thy pilgrim way:
Remember thou art not thine own;
Remember thou art not alone;
For GOD to thee thy being gave;
And JESUS died thy life to save;
And all around are those who need
Thy love in thought, and word, and deed.
Thou hast a place in Heaven's plan;
Bring praise to GOD and good to man.

1. Do all to glorify thy GOD:
2. Tread in the path thy Saviour trod.
3. Fear lest thy soul for ever die:
4. Thy flesh keep down and mortify.
5. In penitence forsake thy sin:
6. Each heavenly virtue strive to win.
7. Flee from the place of endless pain,
8. Press on the heavenly rest to gain.
9. Make ready for eternity:
10. Use well each hour that passes by.
11. With deeds of love thy life adorn;
12. The world's temptations learn to scorn.
13. Fight bravely with the powers of hell:
14. Beat down the passions that rebel.
15. Live to meet death without a fear—
16. To meet thy Judge with conscience clear.

T. B. P.

Ejaculations.

Going out. O send out Thy light and Thy truth, that they may lead me.

Going to Church. LORD, I have loved the habitation of Thy house.

At Work. Labour is sweet, for Thou hast toiled.

Thinking. O let not mine heart be inclined to any evil thing.

Talking. Set a watch, O LORD, before my mouth.

Actions of the Day. Let me not be occupied in ungodly works with the men that work wickedness.

In doubt. Teach me, O LORD, to do the thing that pleaseth Thee.

Tempted. LORD JESUS ✠ save me, help me, keep me.

After a Sin. GOD be merciful to me a sinner.

Sorrow or Loss. Thy will be done. Blessed be the Name of the LORD.

When the clock strikes. LORD, teach me to number my days.

Aspirations.

May Thy death, LORD JESUS, be the life of my soul!

LORD JESUS, live in me, and let me live in Thee!

LORD JESUS, be Thou my Saviour, now and at the hour of my death!

LORD, teach me to love Thee with all my heart, with all my mind, with all my soul, and with all my strength.

The LORD make me pure in my thoughts, kind in my words, wise in my deeds, obedient to His laws, and thankful for His favours.

LORD, keep me from all sin and danger this day.

LORD, make my service acceptable to Thee while I live, and my soul ready for Thee when I die.

Teach me, LORD, to submit my desires to reason, my reason to faith, and my whole self to Thee.

In all my ways I desire to acknowledge Thee: do Thou O LORD, direct my paths.

LORD, command what Thou pleasest, and let it be my pleasure to do what Thou commandest.

O LORD, my GOD; call me, that I may come to Thee; fix me, that I may not leave Thee.

LORD, teach me to trust Thy care, to be resigned to Thy will, and to do Thy work.

May the will of GOD, which is most high, most just, and most deserving of all love, be done, praised, and exalted for ever above all things!

Praise be to GOD, peace to the living, and rest to the dead.

LORD, blessed be Thy patience, that endures so long: blessed be Thy grace that delivers at last.

The LORD grant me a share in the happiness of the world to come; and His will be done in all that happens to me in the present world.

In Heaven with Thee, LORD, let me be;
On Earth my heaven's alone in Thee.

Prayers.

GOD be in my head and understanding.
GOD be in my eyes and in my seeing.
GOD be in my mouth and in my speaking.
GOD be in my heart and in my thinking.
GOD be at my end and my departing.
     Amen.

LORD be Thou
Within me, to strengthen me;
Without me, to keep me;
Above me, to guard me;
Beneath me, to uphold me;
Before me, to guide me;
Behind me, to forward me;
Round me, to defend me.

O my LORD GOD, grant me
In my heart to desire Thee;
Desiring Thee, to seek Thee;

Seeking Thee, to find Thee;
Finding Thee, to love Thee;
Loving Thee, to follow Thee.

 LORD, let me ever
Run the race set before me,
Walk in Thy ways,
Stand in Thy grace,
Sit at Thy feet,
Kneel in devotion,
Fall down in adoration, and
Lie down in Thy peace.

 LORD, may I at last
Sleep in Thee,
Wake up in Thy likeness,
Rise by Thy power, and
Reign in Thy glory,
for JESUS CHRIST'S sake. Amen

 Blessed JESU! put
Thy Innocence between my soul and my impurity:
Thy Obedience between my soul and my iniquity:
Thy Agony between my soul and my impiety:
Thy Priesthood and Sacrifice between my soul and my guilt:
Thy Passion between my soul and my punishment:
Thy Intercession between my soul and my indevotion:
Thy Kingdom and Conquest between my soul and my enemies.

 For what Thou didst and what Thou sufferedst, O! my dearest Saviour, O! my best of Masters, was done and suffered in my stead, and for my benefit. Amen.

Hymns.

Shine on our souls, Eternal GOD,
 With rays of beauty shine!
O let Thy favour crown our days,
 And all their round be Thine!

Did we not raise our hands to Thee,
 Our hands might toil in vain;
Small joy success itself could give,
 If Thou Thy love restrain.

With Thee let every week begin,
 With Thee each day be spent;
For Thee each fleeting hour improved,
 Since each by Thee is lent.

Thus cheer us through this desert road,
 Till all our labours cease;
And Heaven refresh our weary souls
 With everlasting peace.
    Amen.

Pilgrim, are you heavy laden,
 Is your pathway dreary,
Has the long and rugged road
 Made you sad and weary?—
Lean on JESUS, lean on JESUS,
 From your load He'll free you,
To your toilsome journey's end
 Safely He will see you.

Do the winds blow bleak and chilly,

Do the storm-clouds lower,
Is your path beset with foes,
   Mighty in their power?—
Trust in JESUS, trust in JESUS,
   See: He stands beside you,
With His arm outstretched to save,
   How can harm betide you?

Are the friends you loved so truly
   Friends, alas! no longer;
When their love should deeper be,
   Truer still and stronger?—
JESUS loves you, JESUS loves you,
   And He longs to take you
To that Sacred Heart of His;
   He will not forsake you.

Fear not, halt not, faithful pilgrim;
   JESUS doth befriend you;
And, by loving angel guards,
   Will from harm defend you.
When the toilsome march is over,
   Then comes rest and gladness,
With an end to pain and toil,
   Trial, woe, and sadness.
A. J. B.

Why should I fear the darkest hour,
   Or tremble at the tempter's power?
JESUS vouchsafes to be my Tower.

Though hot the fight, why quit the field?
   Why must I either fly or yield,
Since JESUS is my mighty Shield?

I know not what may soon betide,
   Or how my wants may be supplied,
But JESUS knows, and will provide.

Though faint my prayers, and cold my love,
   My stedfast hope shall not remove,
While JESUS intercedes above.

Against me earth and hell combine;
   But on my side is Power Divine;
JESUS is all, and He is mine!

50.—HOURS OF PRAYER.

"Seven times a day will I praise Thee." *Ps.* cxix. 164. The Hours of Prayer are these:—

Nocturns or Mattins, a *night* office, usually said with Lauds.

1. Lauds, a service of *praise*, at daybreak. Chapter 51.
2. Prime, about six o'clock, the *first* hour. Chapter 52.
3. Tierce, at nine o'clock, the *third* hour. Chapter 53.
4. Sexts, at noon, the *sixth* hour. Chapter 54.
5. Nones, at three o'clock, the *ninth* hour. Chapter 55.
6. Vespers, an early *evening* service. Chapter 56.

7. Compline, a later service, *completing* the offices of the day. Chapter 57.

The Seven Hours tell the Acts of the Passion:—
At *Matins* bound; at *Prime* reviled, Condemned to death at *Tierce*,
Nailed to the Cross at *Sext*, at *Nones* His Blessed Side they pierce;
They take Him down at *Vesper-tide*, in grave at *Compline* lay,
Who thenceforth bids His Church observe her sevenfold Hours alway.

51.—MORNING PRAYERS.

In the Name of the + Father, and of the Son, and of the Holy Ghost. Amen.

Our Father, Which art in heaven, Hallowed be Thy Name. Thy Kingdom come. Thy will be done in Earth, As it is in Heaven. Give us this day our daily bread. And forgive us our trespasses, As we forgive them that trespass against us. And lead us not into temptation; But deliver us from evil: For Thine is the Kingdom, The Power, and the Glory, For ever and ever. Amen.

I believe in GOD the Father Almighty, Maker of heaven and earth:

And in JESUS CHRIST His only Son our LORD, Who was conceived by the Holy Ghost, Born of the Virgin Mary, Suffered under Pontius Pilate; Was crucified, dead, and buried; He descended into hell; The third day He rose again from the dead; He ascended into heaven, and sitteth on the right hand of GOD the Father Almighty; From thence He shall come to judge the quick and the dead.

I believe in the Holy Ghost; The Holy Catholic Church; The Communion of Saints; The Forgiveness of Sins; The Resurrection of the Body, And the life everlasting. Amen.

Glory be to the Father, and to the Son, and to the Holy Ghost;

As it was in the beginning, is now, and ever shall be, world without end. Amen.

I laid me down and slept, and rose up again; for the LORD sustained me.

Keep me, O LORD, this day without sin.

Guard my going out and my coming in, henceforth and for ever.

Shew Thou me the way that I should walk in, for I lift up my soul unto Thee.

LORD, bless and help me, that I may every day grow more fit for Thy service. Hear my prayers, pardon my failings, be with me in my work, supply my wants, and give me grace to live in Thy fear all the day long; for JESUS CHRIST'S sake. Amen.

Looking off unto JESUS
　I go not astray,
My eyes are on Him, and
　He shows me the way;
The path may seem dark as
　He leads me along;
But, following JESUS,
　I cannot go wrong.

May the Almighty and Merciful LORD, + Father, Son, and Holy Ghost, bless and preserve us, and bring us to life everlasting. *Amen.*

52.—SECOND MORNING PRAYERS.

In the Name. Our Father.
O wonderful exchange! The Creator of mankind, taking upon Him a living body, has not disdained to be born of a Virgin: *And He being made man. has given to us His Godhead.*

Lo, all things are fulfilled that were spoken by the angel of the Blessed Virgin Mary. *Thanks be to God.*

LORD, shew Thy mercy upon us. *And grant us Thy salvation.*

We beseech Thee, O LORD, pour Thy grace into our hearts; that, as we have known the Incarnation of Thy Son JESUS CHRIST by the message of an angel, so by His Cross and Passion we may be brought unto the glory of His Resurrection; through the same JESUS CHRIST our LORD. *Amen.*

O Lamb of GOD That takest away the sin of the world: *Have mercy upon us.*

LORD of goodness and mercy, Who didst send Thine own Son to a Cross, to bring me to a Crown; and at the price of His most bitter Passion didst purchase my salvation. Let this love of Thine be ever in my heart, and let the fruits of it abound in my life. Teach me to hate sin more than death, because it made Thy Son to die. And may nothing in this life be too dear to me; lest I sin against my Saviour, Who has made me by His death to live.

LORD, let me give up all I have and all I am to Thee, Who gavest Thy Dear Son a sacrifice for me; that I may do Thy will all my days, and may dwell with Thee for ever and ever. *Amen.*

Guide Thou my way,
　Who art Thyself
My everlasting end;
　That every step,
　Or swift or slow,
Still to Thyself may tend.

The blessing of GOD Almighty, the + Father, the Son, and the Holy Ghost, be with us this day, the rest of our lives, and evermore. *Amen.*

53.—NINE O'CLOCK.

In the Name. Our Father.
O Thou Who at the third hour didst send to Thine Apos-

tles the gift of the Holy Ghost: *Take not Thy Holy Spirit from me; but fill me with the riches of His grace, and save me.*

Come, Holy Ghost, fill the hearts of Thy faithful: *And kindle in them the fire of Thy love.*

Send forth Thy Spirit, and they shall be made: *And Thou shalt renew the face of the earth.*

GOD, Who didst teach the hearts of Thy faithful people by the sending to them the light of Thy Holy Spirit: Grant us by the same Spirit to have a right judgment in all things, and evermore to rejoice in His holy comfort; through the merits of CHRIST JESUS our Saviour, Who liveth and reigneth with Thee, in the unity of the same Spirit, one GOD, world without end. *Amen.*

Save and deliver and justify us, O Blessed Trinity. *Amen.*

Blessed be the Name of the LORD. *From this time forth for evermore.*

Almighty and everlasting GOD, Who hast given unto us Thy servants grace by the confession of a true Faith to acknowledge the Glory of the eternal Trinity, and in the power of the Divine Majesty to worship the Unity: We beseech Thee that Thou wouldest keep us stedfast in this Faith, and evermore defend us from all adversities; Who livest and reignest, one GOD, world without end. *Amen.*

We worship Thee, O CHRIST, and we bless Thee. *For by Thy Cross and Precious Blood Thou hast redeemed the world.*

LORD JESUS CHRIST, Son of the Living GOD: Set Thy Passion, Thy Cross, and Thy Death between Thy judgment and our souls, now and in the hour of our death. Give to the living mercy and grace, to the departed rest and peace, to the Church and the kingdom peace and concord, to the sick help and comfort, to our friends and enemies true charity, and to us sinners life and endless glory: Who livest and reignest, with the Father and the Holy Ghost, one GOD for ever and ever. *Amen.*

  Live, JESUS, live;
    And let it be
  My life to die
    For love of Thee;
  And grant mine eyes
    One day to see
  The sweet reward
    Of love in Thee.

May the Sacred Trinity, ✢ Father, Son, and Holy Ghost, bless us and ours, this day and for ever. *Amen.*

54.—TWELVE O'CLOCK.

In the Name. Our Father.

O Thou, Who, at the sixth hour, didst nail the sins of the

world with Thy Body to the Cross *Blot out the handwriting of my sins which is against me, and take it out of the way, and save me.*

We ought to glory in the Cross of our LORD JESUS CHRIST. *Amen.*

O GOD, Who hast ascended Thy most holy Cross, and hast given light to the darkness of the world: Vouchsafe to enlighten, visit, and comfort both our hearts and bodies; Who livest and reignest GOD, world without end. *Amen.*

Blest be that hour,
  When He repaired my loss;
I never will
  Forget my Saviour's Cross.

LORD JESUS CHRIST, Son of the Living GOD, Who for our redemption in the sixth hour didst ascend the cross and shed Thy blood through Thy five wounds, for the remission of our sins: We meekly beseech Thee, that, through the merits of the same Passion we may enter the gate of Paradise; Who livest and reignest GOD, with GOD the Father in the unity of GOD the Holy Ghost, world without end. *Amen.*

  LORD, Who for me
    Didst on the Tree
  Open Thine heart of love:
    My Peace in strife,
    In death my Life,
  O help me from above!

May the glorious ✠ Passion of our LORD JESUS CHRIST deliver us from sorrowful heaviness, and bring us to the joys of Paradise. *Amen.*

55.—THREE O'CLOCK.

In the Name. Our Father.

O Thou, Who at the ninth hour didst taste death for the sins of every man: *Mortify all my members, which are upon the earth, even all things that are contrary to Thy holy will, and save me.*

O LORD JESUS CHRIST, Who hast power over all things, and Whose will none can resist; Who didst vouchsafe to be born, to die, and to rise: By the mystery of Thy most holy Body, and by Thy five wounds, and by the shedding of Thy most precious Blood, have mercy on us, and give us all things needful for our souls and bodies; save us from the temptations of the devil, and from all things that thou knowest to be troubles to us; keep us and strengthen us in Thy service unto the end; give us space for repentance and true amendment of life; make us all love one another; and grant us with all Thy saints in Thy kingdom to have joy without end; Who livest and reignest GOD, with GOD the Father and GOD the Holy Ghost, for ever and ever. *Amen.*

O Saviour of the world,

Who by Thy Cross and Precious Blood hast redeemed us:
Save us and help us, we humbly beseech Thee, O Lord.
Live, O! for ever live and reign,
Blest Lamb, Whom Thine own love has slain;
And may Thy lost sheep live to be
True lovers of Thy Cross and Thee.

The peace of God which passeth all understanding; the + blessing of God Almighty, the Father, the Son, and the Holy Ghost; the virtue of the blessed Cross and Passion of our Lord Jesus Christ be with us now and unto the end. *Amen.*

56.—EVENING PRAYERS.

In the Name. Our Father.
My God, I thank Thee for all the blessings of the past day. I will lay me down in peace, and take my rest; for it is Thou, Lord, only, that makest me dwell in safety. Guard my lying down and my rising up, from henceforth and for ever.

Grant, O Lord, grace, mercy, and life everlasting to all my relations—and friends,—and every one for whom I ought to pray,—or who needs my prayers. Comfort the afflicted.—Give rest to the departed.— [*The line—means, Stop and think.*]

Visit, O Lord, this house, and drive far from it all snares of the enemy; let Thy holy Angels dwell in it, to preserve us in peace; and may Thy blessing be upon us evermore, through Jesus Christ our Lord. Amen.

Jesu, Bleeding Dying Love!
Let me daily die with Thee;
That in Thy sweet Arms above
I may rest eternally.

The Lord + bless and preserve us this night; the Lord make His face to shine upon us, and keep us under the shadow of His wings; the Lord lift up the light of His countenance upon us, and give us peace and rest in Him; now and for ever. *Amen.*

57.—LATE EVENING PRAYERS.

In the Name. Our Father.
O Lord, fulfil all Thy works of grace in me, that I may fulfil all the service that I owe Thee; through Jesus Christ our Lord. *Amen.*

O Heavenly Father, for Thine own great mercies' sake; for Thy truth and promises' sake; for the sake of all the merits and sufferings of the Son of Thy love: pardon all my sins and failings, and receive me into Thy favour. *Amen.*

Lord, forsake us not in the vanishing of our days; but

still continue Thy gracious and fatherly care over us. Be Thou our Light and Defence, our Guide and Guard, through the valley of the shadow of death to the holy hill of Thine honour and our rest; for JESUS CHRIST's sake. *Amen.*

Almighty Father, grant us, we beseech Thee, Thy grace; that we, who reverently make a remembrance of the Incarnation, Nativity, Passion, Resurrection, and Ascension of the Son; and also of the Coming of the Holy Ghost; may, by the grace of the same Holy Ghost, rise from the death of the soul, and with Thee live an eternal life, through JESUS CHRIST our LORD. *Amen.*

Let Thy mighty hand and stretched-out arm, O LORD, be ever our defence; Thy mercy and loving-kindness in JESUS CHRIST, Thy dear Son, our salvation; Thy true and holy word, our instruction; Thy grace and Holy Spirit, our comfort and consolation, this night and for evermore. *Amen.*

LORD, lighten mine eyes: *That I sleep not in death.*

Grant us, O LORD, Thy Light: *That we, being saved from the darkness of our hearts, may come to the True Light Which is Christ.*

Father, into Thy Hands I commend myself, my spirit, soul, and body: *For Thou hast redeemed me, O Lord, Thou God of Truth.*

LORD, save us as we wake, keep us as we sleep: *That we may watch with Christ and rest in peace.*

May the souls of all the faithful departed, by the mercy of GOD, rest in the peace of JESUS CHRIST. *Amen.*

JESU, in my hour of Rest,
  After life's long weary day,
In Thy Arms and on Thy Breast
  Let me breathe my life away!

The ✠ GOD of mercy and peace be with us and ours, and with all that need His blessing, this night and for ever. *Amen.*

58.—THE EVENING.
Daily Self-Examination.

O Fount of mercy,
  Light of heaven,
Our darkness cast away;
  And grant us all,
  Through Thee forgiven,
To see the perfect day.

Did I think of GOD when I awoke?

Did I rise in good time?

Did I say my prayers, fully and devoutly?

Have I remembered GOD's Presence through the day?

How far have I kept my good resolutions?

Have I guarded my heart against evil thoughts?

Have I sinned with my tongue?
Have I done anything wrong?
How far have I yielded to temptation?
Have I gone in the way of temptation?
Have I been diligent, honest, and cheerful in my work?
Have I been moderate in food?
Have I been kind to others?
Have I done anything for GOD's Glory?

Confession.
I confess to Almighty GOD, that I have sinned very much in thought, — word, — and deed.—
May Almighty GOD have mercy on me and forgive me my sins, and bring me to everlasting life.
May the Almighty and Merciful ✠ LORD grant me pardon, absolution, and remission of all my sins.

Renewal of Vows.
Said I not so, that I would sin
  no more?
  Witness, my GOD, I did;
Yet I am run again upon the
  score:
  My faults cannot be hid.
What shall I do? Make vows,
  and break them still?
  'Twill be but labour lost;
My good cannot prevail a-
  gainst mine ill,
  The business will be crost.

O, say not so: thou canst not
  tell what strength
  Thy GOD may give thee
    at the length:
Renew thy vows, and if thou
  keep the last,
  Thy GOD will pardon all
    that's past.
Vow while thou canst: while
  thou canst vow thou may'st
Perhaps perform it when thou
  thinkest least.

Thy GOD hath not denied thee
  all,
Whilst He permits Thee but
  to call:
Call to thy GOD for grace to
  keep
Thy vows; and, if thou break
  them, weep.
Weep for thy broken vows,
  and vow again.
Vows made with tears cannot
  be still in vain.

Then, once again,
  I vow to mend my ways;
LORD, say Amen,
  And Thine be all the praise.

Hymns.
Blest be Thy love, dear LORD,
  That taught us this sweet
    way;
Only to love Thee for Thyself,
  And for that love obey.

O Thou our souls chief Hope,
  We to Thy mercy fly;
Where'er we are, Thou canst
  protect,
Whate'er we need, supply.

Whether we sleep or wake
 To Thee we both resign:
By night we see as well as day,
 If Thy Light on us shine.

Whether we live or die,
 Both we submit to Thee:
In death we live, as well as life,
 If thine in death we be.

Glory to Thee, Great GOD,
 One co-eternal Three;
To Father, Son, and Holy Ghost.
 Eternal glory be. Amen.

O may my Guardian, while I sleep,
Close to my bed his vigils keep;
His love angelical instil,
Stop all the avenues of ill.

May he celestial joy rehearse,
And thought to thought with me converse;
Or, in my stead, all the night long,
Sing to my GOD a grateful song.

Blessed Angels! while we silent lie,
You hallelujahs sing on high;
You joyful hymn the Ever-Blessed
Before the throne, and never rest.

I with your choir celestial join,
In offering up a hymn divine,
With you in heaven I hope to dwell,
And bid the night and world farewell.

All praise to Thee in light arrayed,
Who light Thy dwelling-place hast made.
A boundless ocean of bright beams
From Thy all-glorious Godhead streams.

The sun in its meridian height
Is Thy darkness in Thy sight!
My soul O lighten and inflame
With thought and love of Thy Great Name.

Shine on me, LORD, new life impart,
Fresh ardours kindle in my heart;
One ray of Thy all-quickening light
Dispels the sloth and clouds of night.

LORD, lest the tempter me surprise,
Watch over Thine own sacrifice;
All loose, all idle thoughts cast out,
And make my very dreams devout.

Praise GOD, from Whom all blessings flow;
Praise Him all creatures here below;
Praise Him above, ye heavenly host;
Praise Father, Son, and Holy Ghost. Amen.

Five Parts of Evening Prayer.
1. Give thanks to GOD.
2. Beg light.

3. Search well thy soul.
4. Ask pardon for thy faults.
5. Check sin's control.

Night Thoughts.

Omnipresent God! Whose aid
  No one ever asked in vain;
Be this night about my head,
  Every evil thought restrain:
Lay Thy hand upon my soul,
  God of my unguarded hours;
All my enemies control,—
  Hell, and earth, and nature's powers.

O Thou jealous God! come down,
  God of spotless purity;
Claim and seize me for Thine own,
  Consecrate my heart to Thee:
Under Thy protection take:
  Songs in the night season give;
Let me sleep to Thee and wake;
  Let me die to Thee and live.

Only tell me I am Thine
  And Thou wilt not quit Thy right;
Answer me in dreams divine,
  Dreams and visions of the night:
Bid me even in sleep go on,
  Restlessly my God desire;
Mourn for God in every groan,
  God in every thought require.

Loose me from the chains of sense,
  Set me from the body free;
Draw with stronger influence
  My unfettered soul to Thee;
To me, Lord, Thyself reveal;
  Fill me with a sweet surprise,
Let me Thee, when waking, feel,
  Let me in Thy image rise.

When in the night I sleepless lie
  My soul with heavenly thoughts supply;
Let no ill dreams disturb my rest,
  No power of darkness me molest.

The faster sleep our senses binds
  The more unfettered are our minds;
O may my soul, from matter free,
  Thy loveliness unclouded see!

My soul, when I shake off this dust,
  Lord, in Thy arms I will entrust;
O make me Thy peculiar care,
  Some mansion for my soul prepare.

As every night lays down our head,
  And morning opes our eyes;
So shall the dust be once our bed,
  And so we hope to rise:
To rise and see Thy beauteous light
  Spring from those eyes of Thine;

Not to be checked by any night,
But clear for ever shine.

Ejaculations.

Evening. O JESUS, keep me in Thy sight; and save me through the coming night.

Night. Through life's long day, and death's dark night, O gentle JESUS, be my Light.

Lying down to sleep. ✝ O LORD, in Thy dear love fit me for perfect Rest above.

The Last Thought. How sweet to rest for ever on my Saviour's breast!

At any time, Day or Night. My Father, Thou art the Guide of my youth.

Or,

Thou art my Father, my GOD, and my strong salvation.

Let such as love Thy salvation say alway—
THE LORD BE PRAISED.

In some cases Part IV. may be a sufficient Manual of Devotion for Private and Family use. Prayers from Chapters 52, 53, and 54 can be said at Family Prayer in the Morning; and Prayers from Chapters 55 and 57 in the Evening—all present saying "Amen," the parts printed like *Amen*, and the short Hymns.

The following Psalms may be said before the LORD's Prayer in Chapters 51-57:—

Chapter. 51. 52. 53. 54. 55. 56. 57.
Psalm. 67. 117. 121. 125. 126. 138. 13.

See Note at the end of Part VI.

PART V.—DAILY PRAYERS FOR A WEEK.

"To search out a Resting-place for them."—*Numbers* x. 33.

59.—SUNDAY MORNING.

In the Name of the ✠ Father, and of the Son, and of the Holy Ghost. Amen.

Our Father, Which art in Heaven, Hallowed be Thy Name. Thy Kingdom come. Thy will be done in Earth, As it is in Heaven. Give us this day our daily bread. And forgive us our trespasses, As we forgive them that trespass against us. And lead us not into temptation; But deliver us from evil: For Thine is the Kingdom, the Power, and the Glory, For ever and ever. Amen.

O Sun of Righteousness, Who this day didst rise for me: Shine now and ever with Thy grace and mercy upon me. Raise me, O LORD, at the last day to life everlasting.

O GOD, Who hast of Thy mercy given me to see the light of this holy day: Make me careful to do the duty of it. Grant me rightly to present myself unto Thee, and reverently to behave myself before Thee; that I may come with fruit and favour from Thee; for JESUS CHRIST'S sake. Amen.

LORD, speak in such manner to my soul, that I may hear and obey Thee. Make known to me Thy will, and help me to do it. Teach me and all Christians what Thou art to us, and what we ought to be to Thee.

Give me grace to hear and read Thy Holy Word with reverence, giving up my own understanding and will to Thine. Cause me to believe what Thou hast said, to do what Thou hast commanded to fear what Thou hast threatened, and to love what Thou hast promised.

I beseech Thee to send down upon the Clergy, especially ———— Thy heavenly blessing; that, faithfully fulfilling their course, they may receive a crown of righteousness.

O GOD, the Father of our LORD JESUS CHRIST: Have mercy upon the whole Church and on her children; that we may, with one heart, love, confess, and adore Thee for ever; through JESUS CHRIST our Saviour. Amen.

The LORD ✠ bless me and preserve me this day; the LORD make His face to shine upon me, and keep me under the shadow of His wings; the LORD lift up the light of His countenance upon me and give me peace; now and for ever. Amen.

60.—SUNDAY EVENING.

In the Name. Our Father. [*As on Sunday Morning.*]

My GOD and Father, look in mercy upon me. Cast not out my prayer. Forgive my sins; give me grace to live a godly life; help me to do good unto all men; teach me to please Thee in all things.

Grant me by the ways of Thy grace to come to the home of Thy glory. Teach me so to do Thee service on earth, that Thou mayest give me Thy salvation in heaven; for JESUS CHRIST'S sake. Amen.

O LORD, cleanse and defend Thy Church, and grant that all Christian people may love one another as the disciples of CHRIST.

O CHRIST, Head of Thy Body the Church: Preserve the branch of Thy Church Which Thou hast set up amongst us. Forgive our sins, build up her walls, and prosper Thy work at all times.

Let all that sincerely seek the truth be led into it by Thy Holy Spirit; and to all that are without instruction give a greater measure of Thy grace,

O Sun of Righteousness, keep me from outer darkness. Let me so sleep in Thy peace, that I may be ever ready to arise, and meet Thee in Thy glory.

The LORD ✠ bless and preserve me this night; the LORD make His face to shine upon me, and keep me under the shadow of His wings; the LORD lift up the light of His countenance upon me, and give me peace and rest in Him; now and for ever. Amen.

61.—MONDAY MORNING.

In the Name. Our Father.

O Merciful GOD, I am very sorry for all my sins. I grieve that I have offended Thee; and I hope to receive Thy pardon through JESUS CHRIST. I will try to love and serve Thee better. Help me to do what is right, and strengthen me in my good resolves; to the glory of Thy Holy Name, and the salvation of my soul; for JESUS CHRIST's sake. Amen.

Almighty GOD, I beseech Thee, give me grace so to govern my thoughts this day, that I may be kept from all evil words and deeds. Save me from the sins to which I am most easily led, or may be most tempted. May my soul and body be kept pure and without stain before Thee; that, when the hour of their parting shall come, they may be ready for Thee; through the merits and mercies of JESUS CHRIST our LORD. Amen.

O GOD of Peace, let me so live according to my rule, that I may have peace with my conscience; and let my rule of life be so made according to Thy will, that I may have peace with Thee; through JESUS CHRIST our LORD. Amen.

LORD, I pray for my country. Our sins cry to Thee: pardon them. Thy mercies have been great: remember them. Let the light of Thy countenance shine upon us, and give us the blessing of peace; for JESUS CHRIST'S sake. Amen.

May the Sacred Trinity, + Father, Son, and Holy Ghost, bless me and mine, this day and for ever. Amen.

62.—MONDAY EVENING.

In the Name. Our Father.

O Divine Spirit of Truth, give light to my mind, bring to my remembrance the sins that I have committed this day, and give me true godly sorrow for them all.

May I always have grace and courage to fear none but Thee, and nothing but that wherein I offend Thee.

Fix in my heart a firm purpose and habit of leading a Christian life. May it be my constant care to do everything that I know will please Thee, and to avoid everything that I know will displease Thee; for JESUS CHRIST'S sake. Amen.

Have mercy on all who have not yet learned to fear and love Thee. Let the light of Thy grace shine upon them; and so touch their hearts, that they may see the beauty of Thy truth and be glad to embrace it. Thou, LORD, knowest the conditions, desires, and wants of all men. Suit Thy graces and blessings to each man's needs of soul and body; for JESUS CHRIST'S sake. Amen.

LORD, hear my prayers; pardon my sin and weakness; give me what is needful for soul and body; and keep me ever under Thy care.

May the Sacred Trinity, + Father, Son, and Holy Ghost, bless me and mine, this night and for ever. Amen.

63.—TUESDAY MORNING.

In the Name. Our Father.

LORD, Thou hast given me life, and Thou preservest my life from day to day. Thou hast kept me to this hour: leave me not, neither forsake me. LORD, help me always to feel Thy presence and rejoice in it. Suffer me not to seek, to know, to love, or to keep anything that may separate me from Thee. Let goodness and mercy follow me all the days of my life in this world, that I may enjoy a long life with Thee in Heaven; for JESUS CHRIST'S sake. Amen.

O LORD JESUS, I beseech Thee, of Thy great love quicken in me that which is dead; restore to me that which is lost; raise up in me that which is fallen; make perfect in me that which is wanting. Fill me with Thy grace; settle me in Thy faith; make me like unto Thyself. Draw my heart away from all things below; and so work in me, that both in soul and body I may be holy and may live to Thy glory, world without end. Amen.

O Holy Spirit of Grace, sanctify my heart, govern my tongue, guard my eyes, cleanse my hands, guide my feet, and order the whole course of my life.

LORD, grant unto all sinners a true sense of their state, a fear of Thy judgments, grace and strength to break their bonds; for JESUS CHRIST'S sake. Amen.

The + GOD of mercy and peace be with me and mine, and with all that need His blessing, this day and for ever. Amen.

64.—TUESDAY EVENING.

In the Name. Our Father. Gracious Father, without Thee I can do nothing but sin: only by Thy help can I confess my sin, and seek pardon as I ought. I was born in sin. Thou didst cleanse my soul in Holy Baptism. But I have sinned against Thy grace. Teach me to see and confess, to hate and forsake all my sins; that I may find mercy and salvation in JESUS CHRIST. Amen.

LORD, it is of Thy mercy that I have life and health. Make me so to use these gifts to Thy honour, that Thou mayest continue to bestow them. Visit me not in Thine anger, but save me in Thy mercy; for JESUS CHRIST'S sake. Amen.

LORD, I confess that by reason of my wanderings I have lost all claim to Thy care. I have not been, as I ought, a dutiful Child; yet be Thou, as Thou ever art, a merciful Father. Give me Thy pardon for sinning against Thee, Thy grace to serve Thee better, and Thy care to preserve me this night and evermore.

Be gracious, O LORD, to all that are in affliction of mind or body, or in any pressing need; all desolate widows and fatherless children; all that call upon Thee in their distress, and have none to help them; for JESUS CHRIST'S sake. Amen.

The ✠ GOD of mercy and peace be with me and mine, and with all that need His blessing, this night and for ever. Amen.

65.—WEDNESDAY MORNING.

In the Name. Our Father.

LORD, forgive the sins of which my conscience is afraid; and turn away the judgments which I have most justly deserved.

May Thy restraining grace preserve me from the temptations of an evil world, from the evil of my own nature, and from the evil customs of the age.

Gracious Father, I pray Thee, be with me in all the course of my life, and in all the duties of my calling. Suffer no malice to hurt me, no deceit to mislead me, no violence to oppress me, no falsehood to betray me. Prevent, I beseech Thee, what I cannot foresee; overcome what I cannot withstand; unmask what I do not fear. Especially be with me at this time, and preserve me from all evil; that I may for ever glorify Thee and be safe in the merits and mercies of JESUS CHRIST, my only LORD and Saviour. Amen.

I pray to Thee, O LORD. for my enemies; not for vengeance but for mercy: that Thou wouldest change their hearts by Thy grace, or restrain their malice by Thy power; for JESUS CHRIST'S sake. Amen.

The blessing of GOD Almighty, the ✠ Father, the Son, and the Holy Ghost, be with me this day, the rest of my life, and evermore. Amen.

66.—WEDNESDAY EVENING.

In the Name. Our Father.

O GOD, Who hast made the day for labour and the night for rest: Let Thy Son's Blood cleanse me from this day's guilt; that I may sleep in Thy peace, and rise again refreshed and preserved by Thy favour; through JESUS CHRIST our LORD. Amen.

O LORD, for Thy mercies' sake, I pray Thee, forgive me the bad use I have made of the blessings of Thy goodness. For Thy glory and my comfort, give me grace so to use them for the future, that Thou mayest not take them from me; for JESUS CHRIST'S sake. Amen.

Let the law of Thy Gospel be the rule of my life; let me not only know Thy will, but also do it, by the help of Thy grace, without which I can do nothing.

O merciful GOD, save all that are in trouble; deliver the outcast and poor; help them to right that suffer wrong; let the sorrowful sighing of the prisoners come before Thee; according to the greatness of Thy power preserve those that are appointed to die; have pity upon all that are now breathing their last; give ease to those in pain and sickness; give supply to those that want; give grace to the wicked; and grant us Thy salvation; through the merits of JESUS CHRIST. Amen.

LORD, save and keep all that are near and dear to me and to Thee, this night and evermore; for JESUS CHRIST's sake. Amen.

The blessing of GOD Almighty, the + Father, the Son, and the Holy Ghost, be with me this night, the rest of my life, and evermore. Amen.

67.—THURSDAY MORNING.

In the Name. Our Father.

Have mercy upon me, O GOD, after Thy great goodness, and give me such a true sorrow for my sins, as shall make me able to use gladly all needful means, be they ever so bitter, for rooting sin out of my soul.

May the good Spirit of GOD assist me! May the LORD give me such a lively sense of His Presence and His mercy, that I may serve Him with my heart as well as with my body, and that my prayers may always be heard for the sake of JESUS CHRIST my Saviour.

O Eternal GOD, Who hast made all things for man, and man for Thy glory: sanctify my body and spirit, my thoughts and intentions, my words and actions; that, doing all things for Thy glory, I may see Thy glory hereafter.

Grant that I may perceive and know what things I ought to do, and also may have grace and power faithfully to fulfil the same.

O GOD, Almighty and Merciful, let Thy Fatherly kindness be upon all whom Thou hast made. Hear the prayers of all that call upon Thee; draw mercifully to Thyself them that never pray for themselves; pity the sighs of them that are in misery; open the eyes of them that are in darkness; give more grace to them that fear and serve Thee; for JESUS CHRIST's sake. Amen.

GOD the Father + bless me; GOD the Son defend me; GOD the Holy Ghost preserve me and mine, this day and for ever. Amen.

68.—THURSDAY EVENING.

In the Name. Our Father.

It hath pleased Thee, O LORD, to add another day to the years of my life, and to keep me from the dangers of an evil world. For these, and for all Thy mercies bestowed upon me from day to day, I bless Thy good and gracious providence; most earnestly beseeching Thee to pardon my offences of the day past, and to grant that they may never rise up in judgment against me.

Enlighten me, LORD JESUS, with the brightness of Thy light; and cast out all darkness from the dwelling of my heart. Restrain my wandering thoughts: fight against them that fight against me. Pour forth Thy grace from above; water my heart with the dew of heaven; lift up my mind; take away the load of sin; raise my desires to heavenly things; and fill my heart with Thy love.

Grant, LORD, to all penitents a true sense of their sins, true repentance for them, and Thy gracious pardon; that their souls may be saved in the day of the LORD JESUS.

May Almighty GOD take me and all that belong to me under His care! May He give His angels charge concerning us! May He keep us in peace and safety, through JESUS CHRIST our LORD!

GOD the Father + bless me; GOD the Son defend me; GOD the Holy Ghost preserve me and mine, this night and for ever. Amen.

69.—FRIDAY MORNING.

In the Name. Our Father.

I will arise and go to my Father, and will say unto Him: Father, I have sinned against heaven and before Thee, and am no more worthy to be called Thy child.

O cleanse Thou me from my secret faults. Consider and hear me, O LORD, my GOD; lighten mine eyes, that I sleep not in deadly sin. O remember not the sins and offences of my youth; but according to Thy mercy think Thou upon me, O LORD, for Thy goodness. A broken and contrite heart, O GOD, shalt Thou not despise.

Give me grace that I may continue in Thy fear all the day long; that I may live and act as in Thy Presence; and that it may be the purpose of my soul never to offend Thee by wilful sin.

Teach me gladly to take at Thy hands good and bad, bitter and sweet, joy and sorrow; and in all things to be heartily thankful unto Thee.

O LORD JESUS CHRIST, Who saidst to Thy Apostles, Peace I leave with you, My Peace I give unto you: Regard not my sins, but the faith of Thy Church, and grant unto her that peace and unity which is agreeable to Thy will: Who livest and reignest GOD for ever and ever.

Have mercy, LORD, on all sinners; turn their vices into virtues; make them lovers of Thee, and keepers of Thy law; that they may be numbered with Thy saints in glory everlasting.

The peace of GOD, which passeth all understanding; the ✢ blessing of GOD Almighty, the Father, the Son, and the Holy Ghost; the virtue of the blessed Cross and Passion of our LORD JESUS CHRIST be with us now and unto the end. Amen.

70.—FRIDAY EVENING.

In the Name. Our Father.

Almighty GOD, Who hast kept me this day from many sins and dangers: I praise Thee for Thy grace and goodness. Forgive me all those things of which my conscience is afraid or ought to accuse me. And grant that the sins which by my frailty have been committed may be more carefully guarded against; for JESUS CHRIST'S sake. Amen.

Give me the victory over all my sins and failings; increase in me the graces of faith, hope, and charity; of humility, meekness, patience, resignation, and all other Christian virtues.

Grant that in all my troubles I may suffer as a Christian, and not grieve as an unbeliever; that I may receive afflictions as punishments due to my past offences, as an exercise of my faith and patience and humility, and as a trial of obedience; and that all things may lead to the good of my soul and to Thy glory.

Give me a true compassion for the miseries of others, that Thou mayest have compassion on me at the last day. Keep me from all idle and vain expenses, that I may have to give to him that needeth.

LORD, help me to pray for those that hate me. Give repentance to them and to me; that Thou mayest forgive us. Shew Thy mercy to us, that we may learn to be kind to one another; for JESUS CHRIST'S sake. Amen.

The peace of GOD, which passeth all understanding; the ✢ blessing of GOD Almighty, the Father, the Son, and the Holy Ghost; the virtue of the blessed Cross and Passion of our LORD JESUS CHRIST be with me, now and unto the end. Amen.

71.—SATURDAY MORNING.

In the Name. Our Father.

O most merciful GOD, I have sinned against Thee; I have abused Thy goodness; I have not been thankful to Thee for Thy patience. Of Thy great mercy give me still the means of grace and pardon, help me to rise from the sleep of sin, work in me true godly sorrow, lead me to repentance and salvation.

Grant me, O LORD, daily to prepare for death, fear the judgment, flee from hell, and come nearer to heaven.

Give me grace so to fight against the enemies of my soul, that I may pass my pilgrimage in Thy fear, and at last enter into Thy glory; through the merits of JESUS CHRIST our LORD. Amen.

LORD, sanctify and forgive all that I have tempted to evil by my words or by my life; and teach in the right way all those whom I have led to error. Let the light of Thy countenance shine on all who have done me good: let them never come into any affliction or sadness, but such as may tend to Thy glory and their good.

In tender mercy remember all sick and dying persons, that they may omit nothing that is needful to make their peace with Thee.

My GOD, I pray Thee let none of them that desire my prayers be without Thy blessing; but defend, comfort, and guide them to their lives' end.

May the Almighty and Merciful LORD, + Father, Son, and Holy Ghost, bless and preserve me, and bring me to life everlasting. Amen.

72.—SATURDAY EVENING.

In the Name. Our Father.

Forgive me, LORD, the sins of my youth and my last sins; the sins of my soul and of my body; my open and my secret sins; my careless and my wilful sins; all things done to please myself and to please others, which have been displeasing to Thee; sins hidden from others and forgotten by me, yet seen and remembered by Thee. LORD forgive me all that Thou knowest, for JESUS CHRIST'S sake. Amen.

O Thou that art the Light Eternal and the Sun of Righteousness, evermore arising and never going down, giving life and food and gladness to all things: Shine upon me in Thy mercy; cast Thy blessed beams upon the darkness of my mind, and the black mists of my sins and errors; for Thou, LORD JESUS, art my Saviour. Amen.

Teach me, O LORD, to number my days, that I may apply my heart unto wisdom; ever to remember my last end, that I may not sin against Thee.

May the souls of the faithful departed, through the mercy of GOD, rest in peace. Eternal rest give to them, O LORD; and let perpetual light shine upon them.

O GOD, my Keeper and Defender: I lay me down to rest, beseeching Thee to save me and mine from all evil. Cleanse me, soul and body; that I may please Thee waking or sleeping. And when I have run all my course in this life, call me to Thyself, and receive me into glory; for my Saviour's sake. Amen.

May the Almighty and Merciful LORD, + Father, Son, and Holy Ghost, bless and preserve me, and bring me to life everlasting. Amen.

73.—ACTS OF DEVOTION.

[*For each Morning and Evening in the Week.*]

SUNDAY MORNING. — *The Presence of God.* My GOD, I believe that Thou art here, that Thou seest me, that Thou knowest all my deeds, every word of my tongue, and the most secret thoughts of my heart.

SUNDAY EVENING.—*Adoration.* Glory be to GOD the Father, my Creator; glory be to JESUS, my Redeemer; glory be to the Holy Ghost, my Sanctifier, my Guide, and my Comforter.—All love, all glory be to GOD most High.—Holy, Holy, Holy, LORD GOD Almighty, which was, and is, and is to come.—Blessed be the Holy and Undivided Trinity, now and evermore. Amen.

MONDAY MORNING.-*Thanksgiving.* My GOD, I give Thee thanks for all Thy goodness to me, for preserving me in many dangers, for granting me many blessings, for allowing me still to enjoy the means of grace and the hope of glory.

MONDAY EVENING.—*Faith.* I believe in GOD the Father, Who made me: I believe in GOD the Son, Who redeemed me; I believe in GOD the Holy Ghost, Who sanctifies me.— I believe in Thee, O LORD; may I believe more firmly.— LORD, I believe; help Thou mine unbelief.—My GOD, I believe in Thee, and I believe all that Thou hast said, for Thou art Faithful and True.— O that I may believe in Thee, O GOD: give me grace to confess Thee before men, and to be stedfast in the faith.

TUESDAY MORNING.—*Hope.* I hope in Thee, O LORD; may I hope more fully.—O LORD, in Thee have I trusted; let me never be confounded.— O that I may put my whole trust and confidence in Thee, and not in anything that I myself can do.—My GOD, I hope in Thee alone for grace, and glory, and all good things: I trust in Thy promises, Thy mercy, and Thy power.

TUESDAY EVENING.-*Charity.* I love Thee, O LORD: may I love Thee more.—My GOD, I desire to give my whole heart to Thee: let Thy love abound in my heart, and in the hearts of all that profess Thy Name: may I always love Thee, and love my neighbour for Thy sake, and lead my neighbour to love Thee. — Teach me, LORD, to love Thee, and to keep Thy commandments.

WEDNESDAY MORNING. — *Contrition.* My GOD, I am heartily sorry that I have sinned against Thee, because Thou art so good. I hate all my sins, because they displease Thee. I firmly purpose to amend my life. I determine not to sin any more. I resolve for the future to avoid all causes, occasions, and dangers of sin.

WEDNESDAY EVENING. — *Humility.* LORD, I am nothing, and have nothing of my own, I am less than the least of all Thy mercies. Despise not the work of Thine own hands. Thou knowest that I cannot of myself keep from evil, or do anything that is good. I therefore pray Thee to strengthen my weakness, that I may not sin any more.

THURSDAY MORNING.—*Desire.* When shall I come to appear before the Presence of GOD. O send out Thy light and Thy truth, that they may lead me, and bring me unto Thy holy hill, and to Thy dwelling.

THURSDAY EVENING.—*Joy.* LORD, my trust is in Thy mercy, and my heart is joyful in Thy salvation. I will sing of the LORD, because He hath dealt so lovingly with me.

FRIDAY MORNING.—*Patience.* By the love of Thy Cross, O JESU, I live; in that only will I glory; that above all things will I learn to know; that before all things will I prize: by the love of Thy Cross will I take up my cross, and follow Thee; and, when Thy love calls me to it, I will suffer for Thee, as Thou hast suffered for me.

FRIDAY EVENING.—*Oblation.* O my GOD, I desire to give myself to Thee: all that I have and all that I am I offer to Thy service. LORD, sanctify me wholly; that my spirit, soul, and body may become Thy temple. O do Thou dwell in me, and be Thou my GOD, and I will be Thy servant.

SATURDAY MORNING.—*Forgiveness of Injuries.* LORD, I freely forgive all who have ever done me any harm; and I am ready, as far as I can, to make amends to all whom I have injured in any way. Let me learn, O LORD, from Thee, not only to forgive my enemies, but also to seek to do them good.

SATURDAY EVENING.—*Resignation.* Father, I commend myself, with all I love, to Thy care; and I desire to submit cheerfully to all Thy will concerning me. Guide me on earth by Thy counsel, and receive me in heaven with glory.

74.—RULE OF LIFE.

Remember that your life is a race, a battle, and a journey; and that on each day a part of this work must be done.

Do not waste your morning in sleep or idleness. If you have nothing else to do, you have to serve GOD, to do good to your neighbour, and to save your own soul.

Let your waking thoughts be praise and thanksgiving. Rise from your bed with an Act of Adoration.

As you dress, remember that your soul needs continual washing and "durable clothing"—that your holy religion must be not only the garment of your soul, but even the ornament of all your actions.

When you say your Morning Prayers in the usual place, give glory to GOD; thank Him for preserving you; offer to Him all your thoughts and words and deeds; confess your sins with godly sorrow; pray for what you need; bring before GOD the wants of those for whom you should pray; and read a portion of GOD'S Holy Word.

Before you leave your room think a little while of what you have to do—your business, trials, temptatations—and make resolutions.

Try to attend the Holy Eucharist, or some other office of the Church; also Family Prayers.

Say Grace at meals; do all things in the name of the LORD JESUS; and commend yourself often to GOD.

Be obedient to those set over you, considerate to those beneath you, and kind to all.

Throughout the day avoid idleness, and too eager zeal for the things of this life.

Engage in no unlawful business or employment: do not know a wicked person, so as to make him an associate.

Often renew your resolves not to sin against GOD.

Keep in mind that GOD is always present, and that both good and bad angels are always near.

Guard your eyes, your ears, and your tongue.

Let no bad thoughts get into your heart: resist them at once when they come to you.

When you sin, pray for help and pardon.

Use short prayers often. Say a few words in your heart when you begin and end your work, when you are tried, or troubled, or tempted, or in any doubt.

Always have something to do; try to take pleasure in doing good to others, especially to their souls.

When you fail, blame yourself: when you succeed, thank GOD.

Before you go to rest at night, think of the day that is

past, examine yourself, give thanks to GOD: Say your prayers devoutly, think of your last end, commend yourself and yours to GOD'S keeping.

Make religion the business of your life, your study, and chiefest care. Happy evenings follow well-spent days.

75.—SPECIAL PRAYERS.

Head of a Family.

My GOD, Thou knowest that I cannot guide the house except Thou guide me. Let me be careful to give all their dues, that I may receive their duty. Teach me so to rule, and them so to obey, that all things may be done in Thee and for Thee, and that all may reign at last with Thee; through the merits of Him, of Whom the whole family in heaven and earth is named, the great and gracious Master of us all, JESUS CHRIST our LORD. Amen.

Husband.

O gracious Father, Maker and Preserver of heaven and earth, Who in the beginning didst institute Matrimony, thereby foretelling the mystical union of the Church with our Saviour CHRIST: I humbly beseech Thee to give me the assistance of Thy grace, that I may live according to Thy commandments with my wife, whom Thou hast given me for my help and comfort in this world. Teach me to love her as CHRIST loveth His Church, and to cherish her as mine own body. Grant that we may live in peace without debate, in unity without discord. Give us, O LORD, discreet hearts and understanding minds [to bring up our children Christianly and virtuously in Thy faith and fear.] Thou knowest what is needful for us: help us to maintain ourselves according to the rank of life in which Thou of Thy goodness hast placed us. Grant this, O LORD, for JESUS CHRIST'S sake. Amen.

Wife.

O merciful and loving LORD GOD, Who, in the beginning, didst take Eve out of the side of Adam, and give her and him for a helper: Grant me to love my husband with a true and pure love, acknowledge him as my head, and obey him in all good things. Save me from the wiles of the devil and from the vain fashions of the world. May the enemy never lead me astray, or make me a snare to my husband. Grant that we may live in peace without debate, in unity without discord. Give us, O LORD, discreet hearts and understanding minds, [to bring up our children Christianly and virtuously in Thy faith and fear.] May we strive to please one another in all things; and above all things to please Thee. Grant this, O LORD, for JESUS CHRIST's sake. Amen.

Father or Mother.

LORD, I plead with Thee for my children. Help them with grace to be Thy children; and bless me with grace, by good example and training to keep them Thine. Let me now commend them and myself to Thy Fatherly protection. May we take care to do Thy will, and cast all further care upon Thee; for Thy dear Son's sake, JESUS CHRIST our LORD. Amen.

O GOD, the Father of our LORD JESUS CHRIST: For Thy dear Son's sake, bless my children with healthful bodies and understanding souls and sanctified hearts; that they may remember their Creator all their days. Let Thy grace preserve them from the temptations of this evil world. May I never be wanting in any part of my duty to them; but carefully instruct them in the faith and duty of a Christian life, show them their faults, and correct them in love. O be Thou, O GOD, their Father and portion in this world and in the world to come; for the sake of Thy beloved Son, JESUS CHRIST our LORD. Amen.

First Prayers.
For a Little Child.

O my GOD, teach me to love Thee.
O my GOD, help me to pray.
O my GOD, keep me from sin.
O my GOD, I give Thee my heart.

Gentle JESUS, meek and mild,
Look upon a little child,
Pity my simplicity,
Suffer me to come to Thee.

Our Father, Which art in Heaven, Hallowed be Thy Name. Thy Kingdom come. Thy will be done in Earth, As it is in Heaven. Give us this day our daily bread. And forgive us our trespasses, As we forgive them that trespass against us. And lead us not into temptation; But deliver us from evil: For Thine is the Kingdom, the Power, and the Glory, For ever and ever. Amen.

My Father in Heaven, bless my father and mother, my brothers and sisters, my teachers and friends; bless me, and make me a good child; and keep us all safe this day [or night]. through JESUS CHRIST our LORD. Amen.

O LORD JESUS CHRIST, Who wast for me a little child: Teach me to be good and holy like Thee. Help me to love and obey my father and my mother; that I may be a child of their love, and an heir of their blessing. Amen.

Hear me, Saviour, meek and mild;
Hear and save a little child.

Farmer.

O LORD, I toil in vain, if Thou dost not bless me. Let me reap what I sow, and receive what I hope for; taking care to employ honestly to my comfort, others' good, and Thy glory what I reap and receive.

As my labour is Eden-work, let me seek innocency in it and with it, being refreshed by Thy blessing and a good conscience. Help me to plough up the fallow ground of my heart by repentance, to receive into it the precious seed of Thy Word, to ask and wait for the dew of Thy grace; that, in the end of the world, I may be gathered into Thy barn. O Thou great Husbandman of souls, teach me this holy husbandry—so to thrive in grace that I may grow rich in glory, through JESUS CHRIST our LORD. Amen.

Business or work of any kind.

O eternal GOD, guide me in all my affairs, that I may be diligent, just, and faithful in my calling. Bless and prosper my labours, as Thou in Thy wisdom seest most convenient for me; and teach me to be thankful for all Thy mercies.

What I know to be unjust or wrong, let me not do. What I doubt, let me delay, till I can know and do the right. Let neither custom nor the desire of gain lead me against Thy law and my conscience. May I never lose my soul in my work, or give for money of little value what was bought with Precious Blood. May I rather be a beggar in this world, than a bankrupt in the next.

In the way of just dealing Thou canst prosper me. In that good way let me ever depend on Thee; that Thou mayest bless me in all that I do, and make me a partaker of Thy heavenly treasure, through JESUS CHRIST our LORD. Amen.

Servant.

Blessed LORD and Saviour JESUS CHRIST, Who, when Thou wast the Son of GOD, didst take upon Thee the form of a servant: Grant that I may with gentleness of spirit, singleness of heart, and willingness of mind serve those under whom I am placed. Help me to do all things as to Thee and for Thine honour; and to work, not because man sees me, but because Thine eye is upon me. Teach me, for the love of Thee, to do my duty in the state of life to which Thou hast called me; that I may at last be exalted to the happy place where Thou, with the Father and the Holy Spirit, reignest in eternal glory, world without end. Amen.

Meals.

Before a Meal. LORD, bless us and what Thou hast provided for us.

Or,
Thou, LORD, our daily bread dost give,
By Thee our souls and bodies live;
O teach us more Thy love to know—
The love from which our blessings flow. *Amen.*

After a Meal. The LORD be praised for all His bounties.

Or,
Grant, LORD, that we, with daily bread
For soul and body freely fed,
In all Thy gifts Thy love may see,
And use our strength in serving Thee. *Amen.*

Journey.

Before a Journey. Let Thy Presence go with me, O LORD, that I may be safe. Guide me, prosper me, and lead me to the end. Let not my sins follow me; but let Thy mercy put them from me, and Thy grace accept me. LORD, save me and mine, and all that travel by land or sea; for JESUS CHRIST'S sake. Amen.

After a Journey. O GOD, Who hast been with me, and of Thy great mercy hast preserved me: Make me grateful for all that Thou hast done for me, and accept my praises. LORD, bless me and mine; and grant that, by the guidance and assistance of Thy grace, we may at last arrive at the land of everlasting life; to love, adore, and rejoice in Thee for evermore; through JESUS CHRIST our LORD. Amen.

PART VI.—FAMILY PRAYERS FOR A WEEK.

"Come ye yourselves apart into a desert place, and rest a while."—*S. Mark* vi. 31.

76.—SUNDAY MORNING.

In the Name of the ✠ Father, and of the Son, and of the Holy Ghost. *Amen.*

Our Father, Which art in Heaven, Hallowed be Thy Name. Thy Kingdom come. Thy will be done in Earth, As it is in Heaven. Give us this day our daily bread. And forgive us our trespasses, As we forgive them that trespass against us. And lead us not into temptation; But deliver us from evil: For thine is the kingdom, the Power, and the Glory, For ever and ever. Amen.

O GOD, we believe that Thou art here present with us. We are not worthy to come into Thy Presence. But Thou hast called us, and we come to Thee.

LORD, grant Thy servants grace to obey Thee, and help us to give up this holy day to Thy love and service. Pardon our past neglects; take away all the sins of the past week; and let Thy Presence guide us every day.

O LORD, in Whom we live, and without Whom we die: kill in us all desires of the flesh, and quicken our hearts with Thy holy love; that we may not regard the vanities of the world, but give our love to Thee above all. May our thoughts and words be of Thee, our works and sufferings all for Thee.

O LORD, teach us to observe the times, and love the places of holy worship which Thou hast appointed. Make us diligent in Thy service, and reverent at our devotions. Grant that, as Thy saints and angels in heaven serve Thee without ceasing; so we may, with them and all Thy saints on earth, serve Thee without fainting; till we all come into the presence of Thy glory, and adore Thee for ever; through JESUS CHRIST our LORD. *Amen.*

O merciful GOD, increase, we pray Thee, the number and the graces of such as are jealous for Thy glory and for the salvation of sinners. Shew them the true way of teaching, and let Thy blessing be upon their pious work.

Bless Thy Holy Catholic

Church, spread upon the face of the whole earth. Grant that we may all be, and continue to be, living faithful and obedient members, under CHRIST the Head, in that Church, all the days of our lives and at the hour of our death.

Be pleased to hear the prayers of Thy Church; and grant that, all errors and evils being taken away, she may serve Thee in peace and safety, through JESUS CHRIST our Saviour. *Amen.*

The LORD ✚ bless us and keep us this day; the LORD make His face to shine upon us, and keep us under the shadow of his wings; the LORD lift up the light of His countenance upon us, and give us peace, now and for ever. *Amen.*

77.—SUNDAY EVENING.

In the Name. Our Father. [*As on Sunday Morning.*]

O GOD, Who art the author of all good gifts and the Father of mercies: We, Thine unworthy servants, desire to praise Thy Name for all Thy goodness towards us.

Gracious GOD, Who alone art worthy of all our service: Grant that we may serve and please Thee, as we ought, with all our heart and with all our strength; that, abiding in Thy faith, fear, and love unto our lives' end, we may be made happy for ever in heaven.

Almighty GOD, Maker and Preserver of all things: Help us cheerfully to commit ourselves and all that belongs to us to Thy merciful care. May we ever look up to Thee for what we want, and be thankful for Thy favours. May we never resist Thy dealings with us, nor despise the means of grace which Thou hast appointed for us.

Grant us an interest in all the prayers of Thy Holy Church, which have this day been offered at the throne of grace.

Blessed be GOD, Who gives us what is best for us, keeps us from dangers, and provides for us what we have not deserved! The good LORD make us mindful of our duty; that we, who often learn how we ought to walk and to please GOD, may continue to do so all the days of our lives; through JESUS CHRIST our LORD. *Amen.*

May Thy Good Spirit, O LORD, sanctify, govern, and preserve the Church of England, keep all her members from the spirit of error and delusion, guard her faith against the restless attacks of Satan and his agents, and lead us all in the way of life eternal; through JESUS CHRIST our LORD. *Amen.*

The LORD + bless and preserve us this night; the LORD make His face to shine upon us, and keep us under the shadow of His wings; the LORD lift up the light of His countenance upon us, and give us peace and rest in Him; now and for ever. *Amen.*

78.—MONDAY MORNING.

In the Name. Our Father.

LORD, Thou hast kept us all our lives unto this day. Help us to spend this day and all the days of our lives in Thy fear and love. May we always do Thy will, and please Thee both in will and deed.

Teach us, O gracious GOD, to begin our works with fear, to continue them with obedience, and to finish them with love; and, after all, to sit humbly down in hope, and with cheerful confidence look up to Thee, Whose promises are faithful, and Whose rewards are without end.

Order our steps, O LORD, that we may not stumble at the uneven ways of the world; but steadily go on to our glorious home; neither complaining of the road, nor turning aside from it.

LORD, Thou knowest what is best for us. Give us, we pray Thee, what Thou wilt, as much as Thou wilt, and when Thou wilt. Do with us in all things as Thou seest best, as it shall please Thee, and as is most for Thine honour. LORD, we are Thine: make us ready to do all things that Thou commandest: teach us to live not to ourselves but to Thee.

Supply us and all others with all things that Thou seest to be good; and give Thy blessing to Thy people, for JESUS CHRIST'S sake. *Amen.*

LORD GOD of Hosts, King most mighty, by Whom kings reign, and in Whose hands are the hearts of kings: Grant unto Thy servant Victoria our Queen, continual health of body and soul; that, her heart always inclining to godly counsels, and all enemies being subdued, we may enjoy perpetual peace and brotherly concord.

Finally, we beseech Thee so to guide us at all times, that we may lead and end our lives in Thy faith and fear, and to Thy glory; through JESUS CHRIST our LORD. Amen.

May the Sacred Trinity, + Father, Son, and Holy Ghost, bless us and ours, this day and for ever. *Amen.*

79.—MONDAY EVENING.

In the Name. Our Father.

Pardon, good LORD, all our sins. Make us sorry at our hearts for all the evil that we have done, and give us grace to lead more holy lives.

And now, LORD, we pray Thee, that, as Thou hast dwelt with us this day, it may please Thee to watch over us this night. Keep us therefore, Gracious Father, under Thy care; for unto Thy mercy and protection we commit ourselves; humbly beseeching Thee that, after due rest and refreshment, we may rise with thankful hearts, and return cheerfully to the duties of our callings.

O LORD GOD, Who by the power of Thy word didst bring a glorious light out of darkness: Let the Sun of Righteousness arise upon us, to take away the darkness of our hearts, and save us from the shadow of death; that we may walk in the light of Thy grace here, and rejoice in the brightness of Thy glory hereafter.

O GOD, Whose mercies are without end: We thank Thee for Thy great goodness to us. We pray Thee to continue Thy gifts; and to grant us so much of the blessings of this life as Thou knowest to be good for our souls.

May the Spirit of CHRIST ever live and rule in us; filling our souls with a sincere love of Thee, an earnest desire to please Thee, and a holy dread of offending Thee.

Hear us, Father, when we pray for all men; and hear the prayers of all that pray for us. Let their prayers and ours be acceptable in Thy sight; for the merits of JESUS CHRIST our Saviour. *Amen.*

Keep us under Thy defence and care this night. Make our sleep safe and refreshing. Fit us for our great change; that, having led holy lives, we may in our deaths have comfort and well grounded hope in Thee.

May the Sacred Trinity, ✠ Father, Son, and Holy Ghost, bless us and ours, this night and for ever. *Amen.*

80.—TUESDAY MORNING.

In the Name. Our Father.

O LORD our Heavenly Father, Who hast brought us safely to the beginning of another day: We thank Thee for this and for all Thy mercies. May we live in Thy fear, and in charity with our neighbours. May Thy Holy Spirit direct and rule our hearts, teaching us what to do and what to avoid. May Thy grace ever be with us in all dangers and temptations. Bless all our honest endeavours, and make us content with what Thy providence shall appoint for us; that we may be Thy faithful servants for ever.

Almighty GOD, the fountain of purity and joy, Who by Thy

Word and Holy Spirit dost lead all Thy servants in the ways of peace and holiness: Grant unto us so to repent of our sins, to reform our errors, to watch over our actions, and to do our duty; that we may never break Thy holy laws willingly. May it be the work of our lives to obey Thee, the joy of our hearts to please Thee, the satisfaction of our hopes to live with Thee in Thy kingdom for ever; through JESUS CHRIST our LORD. *Amen.*

May Thy blessing be upon us, upon all that we do, and upon all that belongs to us. Let us never begin any work, or do any thing, on which we dare not ask Thy blessing. And let no worldly business or pleasure turn us away from the things of the world to come.

Bless, we beseech Thee, O GOD, all whom Thy providence has placed over us, whether in Church or State. Give us grace to honour and obey them for conscience sake.

O Everlasting GOD, grant that as Thy Holy Angels alway do Thee service in Heaven, so by Thy appointment they may succour and defend us on earth.

These things, and whatever else our needs, our charity, or our duty obliges us to pray for, we most humbly beg in the Name and for the sake of JESUS CHRIST our Saviour. *Amen.*

The ✝ GOD of mercy and peace be with us and ours, and with all that need His blessing, this day and for ever. *Amen.*

81.—TUESDAY EVENING.

In the Name. Our Father.

Grant, LORD, by the help of Thy grace, that we may perfectly know and truly confess all our sins; and have assured pardon of them all; for JESUS CHRIST'S sake. *Amen.*

O LORD and Heavenly Father, by Thy favour we have come to the evening of another day. We acknowledge Thy great goodness in sparing us when we deserved punishment, in giving us what we need in this life, and in setting before us the happiness of a better life. Shadow us this night, we pray Thee, under the blessed wings of Thy protection, and cover us with Thy mercy. Let not the prince of darkness have any power over us, nor the works of darkness prevail against us. May we be armed with Thy defence, and preserved both in body and soul, through JESUS CHRIST our LORD. *Amen.*

LORD, grant that we, who live together in love now, may live with Thee in joy for ever.

Let us so live in Thy service, that we may die with Thy salvation. What we want of earthly good, give us. What is wrong in us, forgive us. What we need to make us serve Thee, do Thou bestow. May we have grace to seek and see Thy face in JESUS CHRIST our LORD. *Amen.*

Bless the Queen and governors of this land. Let brotherly love increase amongst us, and root out all growing vices. Supply the wants of the poor and needy; help the afflicted, the fatherless, and the widow; save all that suffer under any great sorrow, loss, or sickness; especially all that suffer in a righteous cause.

The + GOD of mercy and peace be with us and ours, and with all that need His blessing, this night and for ever. *Amen.*

82.—WEDNESDAY MORNING.

In the Name. Our Father.

Grant, O Heavenly Father, that as by Thy great mercy we have quietly passed this night, so we may give this day to Thy service. Let all our thoughts, words, and deeds tend to Thy glory and our salvation; for JESUS CHRIST'S sake. *Amen.*

We beseech Thee, O LORD to show upon us Thine exceeding great mercy, which no tongue can worthily express. May it please Thee to save us from all our sins, and from all the evils that our sins deserve. Keep us from evil ways, and lead us in the right way. May we follow after that which is good, and flee from all danger of sin. If we forget Thee, LORD, remember us. If we fall by our weakness, raise us up again by Thy grace. Rule our hearts, keep our tongues, guide our actions, this day and always; for JESUS CHRIST'S sake. *Amen.*

LORD, graciously hear the prayers offered for us by Thy Saints in heaven and by Thy faithful upon earth. Save us from all the snares of our enemies, from wicked men and wicked angels. Help us to be contented with our lot, and to take our trials patiently. In all our passage through this world, and our work in it, suffer not our hearts to be set too much on it and the things that belong to it. Fix our eyes on the hope that Thou hast set before us, that we may make all things tend to it.

Comfort all who want the blessings we enjoy. Give due supplies of mercy to the souls and bodies of all the afflicted.

The blessing of GOD Almighty, the + Father, the Son, and the Holy Ghost, be

83.—WEDNESDAY EVENING.

In the Name. Our Father.

Pardon, good LORD, all the sins that we have this day committed, in thought, or word, or deed, against Thee, or against our neighbour, or against ourselves, for the merits of JESUS CHRIST. *Amen.*

LORD, we bless Thee for the mercies of the past day, and pray Thee to defend us through the coming night; that our souls and bodies may be kept in holiness and safety. Let the changes of day and night keep us in mind of the shortness of our lives. Give us grace to seek and find salvation in this our day of grace; that, when the night of death comes, we may enter into the joy of our LORD JESUS CHRIST. *Amen.*

Save us, good LORD, from our sinful selves, from the love of this present evil world, and from everything that opposes Thy grace or hurts our souls. Stablish us in Thy love; strengthen us to perform Thy will; and settle our faith on CHRIST, the Rock of Ages.

Teach us to rejoice in the good that Thou bestowest upon others; and to receive with humble thanks what Thou bestowest upon ourselves.

Preserve all that travel by land or sea; bless the labours of all honest men; and hear our prayers for all that desire or stand in need of them,—especially those that cannot pray for themselves.

Give Thy grace to all men in all places—to all, high and low, rich and poor, that need it; for JESUS CHRIST'S sake. *Amen.*

The blessing of GOD Almighty, the + Father, the Son, and the Holy Ghost, be with us this night, the rest of our lives, and evermore. *Amen.*

84.—THURSDAY MORNING.

In the Name. Our Father.

We give Thee hearty thanks for all the blessings which, in the riches of Thy mercy, Thou hast poured down upon us; and chiefly for the means of grace and the hope of glory. Thanks and adoration be unto Thee for preserving us from the time of our birth unto this day. Keep us, we pray Thee, on this day and on all the days of our lives from sin and danger. So rule and guide us, that all our thoughts, words, and works may tend to the honour of Thy Name, the good of Thy Church, the discharge of our duties, and the salvation of our souls.

Make Thyself present to our minds, and let Thy love rule our hearts in every place and company to which we may be led this day. Keep us pure in our thoughts, temperate in our pleasures, humble in our opinion of ourselves, charitable in our words about others, faithful in our promises, and just in our dealings.

Supply our wants, and protect us against danger. Make us diligent in business, and give us such success as Thou seest to be good for us.

LORD, leave us not to ourselves; for without Thee we can do nothing that is good. To Thee we look up for grace to know our duty, for willing minds to desire to do it, for strength to perform what Thou commandest, for pardon of our sins, and acceptance of our unworthy service.

May we be careful, above all things, to fit our souls for the pure and perfect bliss, that Thou hast prepared for all that love and fear Thee in the glories of Thy kingdom.

Give all men grace to repent of their sins, and become Thy faithful servants. Teach us all to love as brethren, and be kind to one another, for JESUS CHRIST'S sake. *Amen.*

GOD the Father + bless us; GOD the Son defend us; GOD the Holy Ghost preserve us and ours, this day and for ever. *Amen.*

85.—THURSDAY EVENING.

In the Name. Our Father.

O GOD, we adore Thee, we praise Thee, we love Thee. Thou hast made us, and redeemed us, and sanctified us. Thou hast given us the blessings of this life, the means of grace, and the hope of glory.

O merciful GOD, pardon our offences, correct and amend what is wrong in us. As we grow in years, may we grow in grace. As we draw nearer to our end, may we be more prepared for it.

To Thy mercy in our LORD JESUS CHRIST we humbly commit ourselves this night. Be our Sun to lighten us, our shield to defend us. Grant us, if it please Thee, rest of body and peace of mind. Let the voice of joy and health be in our dwelling.

Give, O LORD, Thine angels charge over us, that neither the devil nor his angels; neither the world nor its vanities; neither evil customs nor the evil that is in our own hearts, may bring evil upon us.

Hear us, O merciful Father of all. Hear our prayers for ourselves and others. Hear the prayers of others for themselves and us. Convert those who pray neither for themselves nor others. Above all, look upon the Son of Thy love, the lover of our souls,

Who maketh intercession for us.

GOD the Father + bless us; GOD the Son defend us; GOD the Holy Ghost preserve us and ours, this night and for ever. *Amen.*

86.—FRIDAY MORNING.

In the Name. Our Father.

O LORD, Who hast kept us from danger by night: Preserve us, we pray Thee, from sin by day. May the Holy Spirit assist us this day and all the days of our lives; that we may walk in the ways of holiness, and at last come to Thy glory; for JESUS CHRIST'S sake. Amen.

Blessed be Thy love that gave Thy Son to die for us and to lead us in the way of happiness. Blessed be Thy patience, that still bears with us, after all our despising of Thy grace; and has added one day more to all the misspent days of our past lives. LORD, help us to love Thee for Thy love, and to cleave to Thee for Thy patience; that we may do Thy work here, and prepare ourselves for Thy Presence hereafter.

Give us grace, so to resist and forsake the desires of the flesh; that we may be able to give ourselves up to the guidance of the Holy Spirit, and be ready to love and serve Thee at all times.

LORD, bless all our honest endeavours with good success; continue to us all the blessings we enjoy; make every condition of life, every blessing we receive, everything that befalls us, a means of bringing us nearer to heaven and to Thee.

We pray for our country. LORD, have mercy upon us, and heal our wounds. Purge away our sins, and the sins of the ages before us; and save us from all their guilt. Take away the sins of peace, that lead to war; and the sins of war, that kill the soul. With our sins remove our woes, and preserve us for Thy great mercies' sake in CHRIST JESUS. *Amen.*

Forgive all our enemies. Give them hearts to fear Thee and to be kind to us.

Comfort all that are cast down. Save all that mourn for their sins. Heal them by the bitter passion and the precious death of JESUS CHRIST our Saviour. *Amen.*

The peace of GOD which passeth all understanding; the + blessing of GOD Almighty, the Father, the Son, and the Holy Ghost; the virtue of the blessed Cross and Passion of our LORD JESUS CHRIST be with us now and unto the end. *Amen.*

87.—FRIDAY EVENING.

In the Name. Our Father.

O LORD GOD, we have sinned, and we are sorry for our sins. We have followed our own desires. We have broken Thy holy laws. May Thy mercy pardon us; may Thy grace help us in time of need; for JESUS CHRIST's sake. *Amen.*

Most gracious GOD, Who daily grantest us Thy favours, and bearest with our faults: Accept, we pray Thee, our humble thanks for all Thy kindness. Blessed be Thy goodness, which has this day given us our food, our health, our work, our friends, and all things needful for our souls and bodies. Adored be Thy love and patience, which have allowed us one day more to amend our lives, and have helped us by Thy Holy Spirit to learn the virtues that are wanting in our souls.

O GOD of Peace, give unity to all those that profess Thy Name. As there is one Head, let there be one Body and one Fold. May the Spirit of Truth guide her doctrine, and the Spirit of Holiness rule the lives of her children. Do Thou, O LORD, govern us; and let us obey Thee: do Thou save us; and let us serve Thee. Let all Christian souls throughout the world be truly Thine; for the sake of JESUS CHRIST, our Saviour and our King. *Amen.*

Bless, O LORD, the rest that we are about to take; and grant that, our bodies being refreshed, we may be able to do Thee better service with our souls and bodies.

The peace of GOD which passeth all understanding; the ✛ blessing of GOD Almighty, the Father, the Son, and the Holy Ghost; the virtue of the blessed Cross and Passion of our LORD JESUS CHRIST be with us, now and unto the end. *Amen.*

88.—SATURDAY MORNING.

In the Name. Our Father.

Accept, O gracious Father, this our sacrifice of hearty thanks for all the blessings of this week, and of all the past days of our lives. To Thee we owe our being and our well-being, all that we are and all that we have. Thy daily mercies have been upon us: our daily praises rise to Thee.

Enable us truly to repent of our faults, and to resolve by Thy grace to correct them all. O let Thine arm be our almighty aid, and then we shall return to sin and folly no more.

Give us grace that we may ever walk as in Thy sight; listen to the voice of conscience in all things; and, fearing to offend Thee, never fall into the sins which we have repented of.

O LORD, Who never failest

to help and govern them whom Thou dost bring up in Thy stedfast fear and love; Keep us, we beseech Thee, under the protection of Thy good providence, and make us to have a perpetual fear and love of Thy Holy Name.

Merciful Father, Who art wont to send Thine Holy Angels to keep and guide Thy servants on earth: We pray Thee to grant that Thy Holy Angels may abide with us at all times, to save us from evil spirits, to keep us from all dangers, and to guide us in safe ways; for JESUS CHRIST'S sake. *Amen.*

Bless all the afflicted members of the Body of Thy Son, wherever they are and whatever be their trial. Send them constant patience or speedy deliverance, as seems best to Thee, and is best for them according to their wants.

May the Almighty and Merciful LORD, ✠ Father, Son, and Holy Ghost, bless and preserve us, and bring us to life everlasting. *Amen.*

89.—SATURDAY EVENING.

In the Name. Our Father.

Almighty GOD and most merciful Father; Give us grace, we beseech Thee, to search our hearts and our most secret thoughts; that we may know how we stand before Thee. Let us never be drawn to do anything that may dishonour Thy Holy Name. Teach us to go on in all good things and in Thy holy service unto our lives' end.

Save, defend, and keep us in Thy fear and love, O Thou GOD of mercy and grace. Give unto us the light of Thy countenance, peace from heaven, health of our bodies, cleansing of our hearts, and salvation of our souls in the day of the LORD JESUS. *Amen.*

LORD, save us from the sad end of the wicked, and from the evil ways that lead to that end. Make us always fear Thy judgments, that we may never feel them; and hope in Thy mercies, that we may never lose them. Bless us with a holy life and a happy death.

May Thy Presence bless every member of this family —those that are here, those that are absent, and those that have departed this life.

May the Holy Angel Guardians, to whose care we have been committed by the Divine goodness, watch over us this night, and defend us from all evil.

Remember, O Merciful GOD, our friends, our relations, and all Thy servants; that they may be partakers of the blessings which we ask for ourselves.

May the Almighty and most Merciful LORD, ✠ Father, Son, and Holy Ghost, bless and preserve us, and bring us to life everlasting. *Amen.*

90.—EIGHT BLESSINGS.
S. Matt. V. 10.

Blessed are the poor in spirit; for theirs is the kingdom of heaven. Blessed are they that mourn; for they shall be comforted.

LORD, hear my prayer. *And let my cry come unto Thee.*

LORD JESUS CHRIST, most pure and mild of spirit, Who didst mourn for our sins and unbelief: Grant us likewise to be pure and mild of spirit, and so to mourn for our offences, that we may be partakers of Thy heavenly kingdom; Who livest and reignest GOD, world without end. *Amen.*

Blessed are the meek; for they shall inherit the earth. Blessed are they that hunger and thirst after righteousness; for they shall be filled.

LORD, hear my prayer. *And let my cry come unto Thee.*

LORD JESUS CHRIST, Whose whole life was nothing but humility and meekness, Who only art our true righteousness: Grant us to serve and honour Thee with humble and meek heart, and in all our life and conversation to desire to be occupied in the works of righteousness, Who livest and reignest GOD, world without end. *Amen.*

Blessed are the merciful; for they shall obtain mercy. Blessed are the pure in heart; for they shall see GOD.

LORD, hear my prayer. *And let my cry come unto Thee.*

LORD JESUS CHRIST, Whose property is to be merciful, Who art always pure and clean without spot of sin: Grant us grace to follow Thee in mercifulness towards our neighbours, and always to have a pure heart and a clean conscience towards Thee, that we may after this life see Thee in Thy everlasting glory; Who livest and reignest GOD, world without end. *Amen.*

Blessed are the peacemakers; for they shall be called the children of GOD. Blessed are they which are persecuted for righteousness' sake; for theirs is the kingdom of heaven.

LORD, hear my prayer. *And let my cry come unto Thee.*

LORD JESUS CHRIST, Who madest peace by the blood of Thy Cross, and Who didst suffer persecution: Grant us grace to keep the peace that Thou hast made, and patiently to bear all persecutions; that we may be called the children of GOD, and may inherit Thy heavenly kingdom; Who livest and reignest GOD, world without end. *Amen.*

91.—GOSPEL LESSONS.

[Arranged for a week.]

Sunday Morning. — "Ask, and it shall be given you; seek, and ye shall find; knock, and it shall be opened to you." —*S. Matt.* vii. 7.

Sunday Evening.—"Whosoever shall confess Me before men, him will I confess also before My Father Which is in heaven. But whosoever shall deny Me before men, him will I also deny before My Father Which is in heaven."—*S. Matt.* x. 32, 33.

Monday Morning. — "All things whatsoever ye would that men should do to you, do ye even so to them, for this is the law and the prophets." —*S. Matt.* vii. 12.

Monday Evening. — "Fear not them which kill the body, but are not able to kill the soul; but rather fear Him which is able to destroy both soul and body in hell."—*S. Matt.* x. 28.

Tuesday Morning.—"Where two or three are gathered together in My Name, there am I in the midst of them."—*S. Matt.* xviii. 20.

Tuesday Evening.—" Come unto Me, all ye that labour and are heavy laden, and I will give you rest."—*S. Matt.* xi. 28.

Wednesday Morning.—"GOD so loved the world, that He gave His only-begotten Son, that whosoever believeth in Him should not perish, but have everlasting life."—*S. John* iii. 16.

Wednesday Evening. — " I am the Light of the world; he that followeth Me shall not walk in darkness, but shall have the light of life."—*S. John* viii. 12.

Thursday Morning.—"I am the Vine, ye are the branches; he that abideth in Me and I in him, the same bringeth forth much fruit; for without Me ye can do nothing."—*S. John* xv. 5

Thursday Evening.—"Watch ye and pray, lest ye enter into temptation."—*S. Mark* xiv. 38.

Friday Morning.—" If any man will come after Me, let him deny himself, and take up his cross daily and follow Me."—*S. Luke* ix. 23.

Friday Evening. — " Not every one that saith unto Me, LORD, LORD, shall enter into the kingdom of Heaven, but he that doeth the will of My Father Which is in Heaven." —*S. Matt.* vii. 21.

Saturday Morning. — " He that endureth to the end shall be saved."—*S. Matt.* x. 22.

Saturday Evening.—"I go to prepare a place for you. And if I go and prepare a place for you, I will come again and receive you unto Myself, that where I am there ye may be also."—*S. John* xiv. 2, 3.

92.—FOR EVERY NEED.

We believe, O LORD, in Thee;
Help our unbelief, that we
More of what Thou art may see.
    LORD, in mercy hear us.

[*Repeat* "LORD, in mercy hear us" *at the end of each verse.*]

We would hope in Thee alone;
Make our hopes be all Thine own,
And in fuller peace be shewn.

LORD, we love Thee, we deplore
That we do not love Thee more;
Warm our coldness, we implore.

Grieving Thee is grief and shame,
Help us more to fear Thy Name,
And our thanklessness to blame.

LORD, to Thee our life we owe,
From Thy love our blessings flow,
To Thyself at last we go.

We adore Thee as our all,
Our support when ills befall,
Refuge when our foes appal.

Foolish, weak, and sad we lie;
Guard us with Thy loving eye,
Be our helper, always nigh.

May Thy Wisdom be our guide;
Comfort, rest, and peace provide
Near to Thy protecting side.

At Thy feet our thoughts we lay,
Make Thine own the words we say,
Make our lives more pure each day.

When oppressed with trouble sore,
Teach our hearts to feel the more
For the pangs our Saviour bore.

What Thou willest may we will,
Nor our own desires fulfil,
For we know not good from ill.

On our darkness shed Thy light
Lead our wills to what is right,
Wash our evil nature white.

Keep us lowly that we may,
Ever watchful, turn away
From the snares our tempters lay.

Fix our hearts on things on high,
Let no evil thoughts come nigh,
Purge from sin our memory.

Turn our eyes from what is vain,
Guide our tongues with careful rein,
That we speak no word profane.

Help us to bewail our sin,
And, in heavenly strength, begin
Daily victories to win.

May we evil lusts subdue,
Long for what is good and true,
And our duty always do.

PART II.

May we true devotion feel
To our GOD, and loving zeal
For our fellow-creatures' weal.

Help us, LORD, in our own eyes
To be lowly, and despise
All the vain world's flatteries.

May we honour great and small,
Help the needy when they call,
And be always kind to all.

May our hearts with love o'erflow
For the wrong, and pain, and woe
JESUS willed to undergo.

CHRIST-like may we insults bear,
And the robe of sorrow wear,
Meeting bitterness with prayer.

May our lips our faith confess,
Teach us, when reviled, to bless,
Conquering by gentleness.

May we selfishness deny,
And the body mortify,
Doing deeds of charity.

Make us wise to do the right
Calm in trouble, brave in fight,
Humble when our path is bright.

Make us earnest when we pray,
Diligent from day to day,
Meaning, doing what we say.

May our words from guile be free,
And our lives the token be
Of our inward purity.

May Thy grace within the soul
Nature's waywardness control,
Guiding towards the heavenly goal.

May we mourn for evil done,
And the ways of evil shun
Until heaven at last is won.

May we prize the Manna sent
For our wondrous nourishment
In the Blessed Sacrament.

Strengthened by that heavenly meat,
Cheered by JESU'S presence sweet,
Make our love and joy complete.

Let the world seem only dross
May we welcome shame and loss,
Willingly endure the cross.

May we feel that here we stay
But for one short fleeting day,
That hereafter is for aye.

May we live, that free from fear
We the angel's call may hear,
And before Thy Throne appear.

May we then, from sin set free,
Rise to heaven to dwell with Thee,
Safe for all eternity.

All we ask is in His Name,
Who to die for sinners came,
JESUS, evermore the same.

Amen.
T. B. P.

The Prayers in this "Part" have been arranged for the use of those who prefer a very simple form of Family Devotion. Others may use, both morning and evening, an order of this kind:—

1. In the Name.
*2. Hymn from this book or the Hymn Book used at Church, or some verses of the Litany in Chapter 92.
*3. Psalm, or portion of Psalm 119.
4. Short Bible Lesson, or Text. See Chapter 91.
*5. Apostles' Creed.
*6. LORD have mercy upon us. CHRIST have mercy upon us. LORD have mercy upon us.
*7. Our Father.
8. Collect for the Week.
9. Prayers from Chapters 52, 53, or 54 in the morning, and from Chapter 55 or 57 in the evening, or Chapter 90.
10. Some of the Prayers as arranged in this "Part."

Nos. 1 to 5 are said standing: Nos. 6 to 10 are said kneeling. All present join in saying or singing aloud the Nos. marked thus *: the reader says the rest; but, in No. 9, all say the words printed like *Amen*, and the short Hymns.

PART VII.—THE CHANGES OF THE WORLD.

"This is the Rest wherewith ye may cause the weary to rest."—*Isaiah* xxviii. 12.

93.—PROSPERITY.

LORD, all that I have is Thy gift. Save me from being proud to others, and from neglecting Thee. Let Thy gifts be a sign of Thy present favour, and of my future joy. If they encourage me to serve Thee, LORD continue them: if they hinder my salvation, LORD remove them. Let me not prosper for a time, and perish for eternity. Give me what may help my well-doing here, and my well-being hereafter. Amen.

94.—ADVERSITY.

LORD, what I suffer is my lot and Thy will. Let me so regard it and improve it; that it may save me from evil, and preserve me for good. May that which seems grievous be Thy rod to reclaim me, Thy staff to hold me up and lead me on, Thy fan to purge me, Thy furnace to prove me. Come and welcome, all adversity in this life, that leads to prosperity in the next! Only let me not be impatient in trial or sinful under it; lest my woe continue in two worlds. LORD, I know that thou dost cross me to crown me. May what I now endure be a badge of favour, a means of grace, and a sign of glory; for my Saviour's sake. Amen.

95.—VARIOUS TRIALS.

Daily Life.

Grant, O GOD, that I may bear all the troubles of this life with a meek and patient spirit; without complaining of what Thou shalt appoint for the punishment of sin and for the salvation of the sinner. I will look to Thee, LORD JESUS; and to Thy patience, when Thou wast in the place of sinners; and this by Thy grace shall be my pattern. Amen.

Anxiety.

O my Saviour, Who didst calm the winds and the sea: speak peace to my troubled spirit, which can nowhere find true quiet and repose but in Thee. Grant that, resigning myself in all things to Thy holy will, I may find peace and happiness in being, leaving, quitting, and suffering whatever Thou shalt appoint. Amen.

Poverty.

LORD, make me by Thy grace to be poor in spirit, that I may be an heir of heaven. Help me to be contented with my lot in this world, and fill me with good things in the world to come; for His sake Who became poor for our sakes. Amen.

Evil Thoughts.

O Almighty GOD, have respect, I beseech Thee, unto my prayers, and deliver my heart from the temptation of evil thoughts; that by Thy mercy I may become a fit habitation for Thy Holy Spirit, through JESUS CHRIST our LORD. Amen.

Suffering for your Religion.

O LORD, the Judge of all the earth, let me suffer as a Christian, though I be treated as a Heathen. Give prayers to my mouth, courage to my spirit, hope to my heart, and peace to my conscience. Forgive the ignorant; give repentance to the malicious. To the judgment of the Great Day I refer my cause. To Thy mercy I commit myself. Help me to endure patiently the wrongful dealings of men; and prepare me for Thy just judgment at last. Amen.

Any Special Sorrow.

LORD, may the trouble I suffer be for the benefit of my soul; that I may for ever rejoice with Thee in that day of bliss that knows no cloud of ill and no end of good for ever. Amen.

96.—RIGHT USE OF TRIAL.

Devotion.

LORD JESUS CHRIST my Saviour, Who in great heaviness of soul before Thy Passion, didst fall down upon Thy face in prayer unto Thy heavenly Father: Grant me, by Thy grace and by the aid of the Holy Spirit, that, in all heaviness of mind and troubles of this world, I may run always by most humble and fervent prayer unto the aid and comfort of my Father in heaven. Hear me, my Saviour, for Thy Name's sake. Amen.

Submission.

O LORD, I give and offer up unto Thee myself and all that is mine, my actions and my words, my repose and my silence; only do Thou preserve and guide me; direct my hand and tongue and mind to things that are good and acceptable unto Thee; and withdraw me from all things contrary to Thy will, for JESUS CHRIST's sake. Amen.

97.—FRIENDS IN TROUBLE.

Sorrow.

O GOD of power and pity: preserve those that are in distress, and show Thyself merciful unto them. Save them from what they suffer and from what they fear. Above all things, give them all the graces and mercies that they need for the saving of their souls. And let all things work together for their good; here if it please Thee, and hereafter according to Thy good pleasure. Amen.

Sickness.

O GOD, by Whose appointment the moments of our life run out: I beseech Thee to receive my prayers for Thy sick servants,—in whose behalf I most humbly beg the help of Thy mercy; that, their health being restored to them, they may return thanks to Thee in Thy Holy Church, through JESUS CHRIST our LORD. Amen.

Sin.

O LORD that delightest not in the death of a sinner: I beseech Thee by Thy grace and providence to stay the course of — who is entered into a way of sin and folly. Let *him* not go on to bring an end of shame upon *himself* in this world, and confusion of face in the world to come. Of Thy great mercy, stop *him* and guide *him*, for JESUS' sake. Amen.

98.—THE TROUBLES OF THE NATION.

LORD, we are in trouble. Thou art just, but we are wicked. Pardon the sin that causes our woes. Pardon the sins of mine that filled up the measure of the whole. Out of evil, work good for us. Out of confusion, make order. O Thou King of kings and Judge of all men, plead the cause of Thy servants. From Thy throne in heaven, own us in our peril and deliver us. Thy power can do it: let Thy mercy grant it; to Thy great honour and our great happiness, for the comfort of body and soul, for us and ours and all that truly love and serve Thee, for all that hold fast Thy true religion in Thee and for Thee. For Thy tender mercies' sake hear us! For the sake of the Precious Cross and Passion of our Saviour help us! For Thine own sake be merciful unto us and bless us. *Amen.*

99.—FOR ALL THAT ARE IN TROUBLE.

LORD JESUS, behold from Thy Holy Place in heaven all upon earth that are in misery of body or soul, and have mercy upon them. Have mercy on all ignorant souls, instruct them: dark souls, give them light: wandering souls, convert them: broken hearts, heal them: the tempted, rescue them: the languishing, revive them: the wavering, establish them: the fallen, raise them up: them that stand, confirm them: those groaning under sin, give them ease: those that go on in sin, stop them. LORD JESUS, Who didst shed Thy Blood for all souls to save them, shed Thy Holy Spirit on all and heal them.

And LORD, have mercy on all those that suffer in body,—on all famishing with want, feed them: bound to beds of pain, loose them: in prison and bonds, visit them: persecuted and oppressed, relieve them: doubting and anxious, settle them: in danger and trial, save them. LORD JESUS, Who didst freely comfort the sorrowful and heal the sick when Thou wast upon earth, hear their cry and help them.

Have mercy upon all, far and near, with me and away from me, every son and daughter of Adam at this time in sorrow or pain upon the face of the earth. Wherever they are, whoever they are, I beseech Thee the GOD of all help and comfort, to give to them whatever help I would desire from Thee or from man, if I were in their state. Take them under Thy care, and supply all their wants, for Thy tender mercies sake. Amen.

100.—HYMNS.

When pleasure shines upon my way,
And all around is bright and gay;
With thankful gladness I can say
    My GOD is Love.

When Satan wields his dreadful power,
And o'er my path dark tempests lower;
I tell my heart in that sad hour
    That GOD is Love.

When over buried hopes I grieve,
When foes are near, and friends deceive;
I faint not, while I still believe
    That GOD is Love.

When dearly loved ones fade and die,
Hope sees unbroken homes on high;
Faith knows that to Eternity
    Our GOD is Love.

When, led by Death's cold shadowy hand,
On Life's extremest bourn I stand;
I'll know that in the unseen land
    My GOD is Love.

I'll yearn for that calm far-off shore,
Where ransomed souls are tried no more
But see what they believed before
    That God is Love.
T. B. P.

Draw me, my Saviour, gently lead
Me where Thy sheep delight to feed:
Draw me, and I will run the race,
Relying on Thy strength and grace.

Draw me with cords of tender love,
Fix all my thoughts and hopes above:
Draw me from earth and all below,
Make me in faith and love to grow.

I am a helpless wandering sheep
Oft on the way I fall asleep:
Jesus! to rouse my slumbering heart
Thy strength and energy impart.

Oh! never from Thee let me rove,
All my distrustful fears remove:
Guide me and lead me in Thy way,
Until I reach eternal day.
S. P.

What time, my soul, sad thoughts prevail,
  And earthly comforts die;
When doubt and fiery fears assail,—
  Lift up Thy trembling eye.

The Son of God, our Priest most High,
  One perfect Offering pleads;
Attentive to the feeblest cry
  He ever intercedes.

For every want, for every care
  In Him is plenteous grace;
Then raise thine heart in fervent prayer,
  And all His mercies trace.
W. P. P.

Blest thought! He *now*, Who wept at Lazarus' grave,
  Who felt, though free from sin, temptation's power,
Regards me, whelmed with sorrow's darksome wave,
  While gathering fears assail in fiery shower.

He, Who of old, on Galilee's dark sea,
  Stilled, with a word, the tempest's sullen roar
Can to my lorn, sad spirit say,—
  Be free!
And waft me gently towards a peaceful shore.

But should this cup, which now seems filled with gall,
  Decreed in wisdom be my portion still,
He can infuse a drop to sweeten all—
  Constraining grace to love His holy will.

And when, unveiled, that
   grateful heavenly theme,
The mystic chain of Providence appears,
Those links will aye reflect
   the brightest beam,
Which unbelief disguised
   with gloomiest fears.

May GOD's best gifts descend
   in balmy shower,
Reviving graciously my
   drooping heart;
May He be with me in each
   trying hour!
Then—all is well! though
   earthly joy depart.
                  W. P. P.

As we tread life's dreary
   journey,
All we suffer on our way
We will offer up to JESUS,
   And with hearts submissive
      say,—
All for JESUS!—what we suffer
   He has suffered long before:
Each dear cross we bear be-
   hind Him
   Shall but make us love
      Him more.

If it is our lot to labour,
   And with toil we feel op-
      pressed;
We will think of Him Who
   laboured
   That our labours might be
      blessed.
        All for JESUS, &c.

When temptations try us
   sorely,
   We shall more than con-
      querors be;
Wrestling as our Saviour
   wrestled,
   Prostrate in Gethsemane.
        All for JESUS, &c.

If through life we're called
   to suffer
Pain, or grief, or misery;
We will gather strength to
   bear it
   From His woe on Calvary.
        All for JESUS, &c.

Death for us shall have no
   terrors,
   He has robbed it of its
      sting:
Through its gloom He bids
   us follow
   To the palace of our King.
        All for JESUS, &c.
                A. J. B.

101.—VARIOUS PRAYERS.

The Soldier's Prayer in time of War.

LORD JESUS, Captain of my salvation: Be my shield by day and my watch by night; that by the guard of Thy goodness I may be safe, and may give Thee glory: LORD, defend the cause of right, and let this war end in peace and happiness, for Thine own sake. Amen.

The Widow's Prayer.
For Herself.

O Merciful GOD, be the husband of the widow. Thou art better than friend, and father, and husband, and all beside.

My heart desires to love and serve Thee: be Thou unto me all, and more than all. Guide my ways; supply my wants; keep me ever near Thee. Let not the world woo me, nor the devil tempt me, nor the flesh betray me; but keep me pure and undefiled before Thee; for JESUS CHRIST's sake. Amen.

For her Children.

O Thou that art the widow's Judge and orphan's Father: I commend to Thy Fatherly care, myself and the children that Thou hast given me. Holy Father, take my children under Thy care, and keep them in Thy fear. Preserve them by Thy grace and mercy. Let me serve Thee in them, and bring them up for Thee. May I never neglect them, nor distrust Thee by over-carefulness. Let my fatherless children find mercy in Thee, O my Father, for Thy Dear Son's sake. Amen.
[*For her Husband, Chapter* 109.]

The Orphan's Prayer.

O Thou ever-living GOD and Father of all; Father of the fatherless: Be my Father now and for ever.
Keep me from want.
Care for me in my cares.
Comfort me in my griefs.
Give angels to guard me.
Defend me from enemies.
Guard me against wrong.
Teach me how to do good.
Convert me in my errors.
Give me enough on earth.
Make me an heir of heaven.
Be my Father, my Guide, and my Salvation. Preserve me on earth: prepare me for heaven. Let me always love and honour Thee as my Father. Thou hast taken me up: leave me not, neither forsake me; but make me like Thy Holy Child JESUS. Amen.
[*For Parents departed, Chapter* 109.]

The Prisoner's Prayer.

O merciful GOD and Saviour JESUS CHRIST, let the sorrowful sighing of the prisoner come before Thee. Give me not over to Satan as a captive, nor to my lusts as a slave. Let Thy mercy free me from the fetters of guilt, and Thy mercy loose me from the bonds of sin. From chains and darkness in the prison of hell, good LORD deliver me. Save me from continuing in sin and delighting in it. Help me to repent of my sins. Teach me to make humble and holy resolutions of amendment. LORD JESUS, save my soul, for Thou hast redeemed me with Thy Precious Blood. Thou wast once in bonds for me: make me Thy freeman in my house of bondage, and remember me when Thou comest into Thy kingdom. Amen.

102.—CHILDBIRTH.
In Travail.

LORD, I have sinned with my first mother Eve. I have often repeated what she did once. I have desired what Thou hast forbidden. I have done evil in Thine eyes, while I did what was pleasing in mine own. I have been tempted to sin, and I have tempted others. But, O LORD, of Thy mercy preserve me in this pain and peril; make haste, O LORD, to deliver me. Remember what my Saviour has suffered for me, save me in my extremity, and let the pains of travail end in the joys of a happy birth; for JESUS CHRIST'S sake. Amen.

After Delivery.

LORD, Thou hast looked down upon Thine handmaid in her distress: I look up unto Thee, and praise Thy Name for Thy goodness. Support me on my bed of weakness, and in due time raise me up; that I may give thanks to Thee in Thy Holy Church, and give back to Thee in Holy Baptism the child that Thou hast given me. Save me and it for Thy mercy's sake. Amen.

After the Baptism of the Child.

Thanks and adoration to Thee, O LORD, for the new-birth of my new-born infant. Thou hast made my child Thine heir; and what was born first to a cross, Thou hast caused to be born again to a crown. LORD, let it be my care to keep my child Thine for ever; through JESUS CHRIST, Thy Son, the Heir of all things. Amen.

103.—SICKNESS.
For Health.

O LORD, when I am well, may I be prepared for sickness; when I am sick, may I be prepared for my last sickness. May I never waste the breath that Thou givest. Teach me to do honour to Thee in my health, that Thou mayest give me comfort in my sickness. Let not sin ever bind me to my bed. And when Thou castest me down, do Thou also lift me up; either to health in this world, or to happiness in a better world; for JESUS CHRIST'S sake. Amen

In Sickness.

O heavenly Father, Who in Thy wisdom knowest what is best for me, glory be to Thee.

LORD, if it seem good in Thy sight, take away this sickness from me, that I may use my health to Thy glory, and may praise Thy Name.

LORD, bless all means that are used for my recovery, and restore me to my health in Thy good time: but if otherwise Thou hast appointed for me, Thy blessed will be done.

I know, O my GOD, that Thou sendest this sickness on me for my good, to correct and to punish, to humble and reprove me; O grant it may have that saving effect on my soul.

LORD, work in me a true penitent sorrow for all my sins past, a stedfast faith in Thee, and sincere resolutions of amendment for the time to come.

Forsake me not, O my GOD, when my strength faileth me: haste Thee to help me, O LORD GOD of my salvation.

LORD be merciful to me a miserable sinner.

O LORD GOD, I know that I must at the last day appear before Thy judgment-seat. O cleanse me from my sins, that I may be found blameless at the coming of the LORD JESUS!

I know, LORD, that Thy judgments are right, and that Thou of very faithfulness hast caused me to be troubled.

LORD, what is my hope! truly my hope is even in Thee.

O Heavenly Father, my hope is wholly in Thy mercy, and in the merits and sufferings of my Saviour; O for JESUS' sake forgive and save me.

O wean my affections from all things below, and fill me with desires after Heaven, and after Thee.

LORD, fill me with Thyself and Thy presence; then call me to Thyself, for the sake of JESUS CHRIST, my Saviour.

Bless me, and I shall be blest;
Soothe me, and I shall have rest;
Fix my heart, my hopes above,
Love me, LORD, for Thou art love.

LORD, behold me chained by weakness to a bed of pain. Let me not fret, even because I belong to Thee—Whose chain I cannot break; Who dost draw me to Thee by this chain; Who for my sin dost justly bind me; Who seest what lies upon me; Who hearest every groan within me; Who knowest when it is best to loose me; Who for my sins mightest bind me in everlasting chains; Who sendest this sickness to save me. LORD, I am Thine, O save me! Make me Thine for ever.

Hear, CREATOR, good and great!
Hear me, SAVIOUR, mild and sweet!
Hear me, HOLY PARACLETE!
  GOD Triune; my GOD, mine All!
SAVIOUR, Who from sin hast freed me,
In life's barren desert feed me,
Through death's darksome valley lead me,
  Homeward to my FATHER's hall.

LORD, Thy hand is heavy upon me: let Thine arm support me. In Thy bosom let me depart if it be Thy will: but, LORD, embrace me with Thy favour, that I may live. May I live out this danger and see Thy deliverance: may I out-live my sins, and do Thee service.

Be merciful unto me, O LORD, that my soul may live. Give pardon to my sin, acceptance to my repentance, strength to my faith, life to my charity, comfort to my spirit, and salvation to my soul; that, whether I live or die, I may be Thine. LORD, cast my sins behind Thy back, and hold me in Thine arms; for Thou art my Hope and Strength, my Refuge, and the Rock of my Salvation! Amen.

My Father, make my pathway plain,
Each unbelieving thought restrain,
And let Thy love my heart constrain,
 Resigned, to say,—
"To live is CHRIST, to die is gain"—
 Thine arm my stay!
   W. P. P.

Eternal Father, I beseech Thee, by the Life and Death of Thy well-beloved Son, and by Thy great mercy, grant unto me that I may persevere in holiness, and die in Thy favour.

LORD JESUS, I beseech Thee, by Thy great love, and by the last words on the Cross, wherewith Thou didst commend Thy Spirit into Thy Father's hands, receive my spirit at the close of my life.

O GOD the Holy Ghost, have mercy upon me; and by Thy holy inspiration strengthen me at all times of my life, and in the hour of my death.

O Most Holy Trinity, One GOD, have mercy upon me, now and unto the end. Amen.

O LORD JESUS, in Thee was found no case of death, and yet Thou didst suffer death for me: I have deserved death; give me grace, O LORD, that I may not fear to die, and that I may be prepared for death. Amen.

104.—THOUGHTS FOR THE SICK.

O LORD, I am sick! Sin makes me. Man's first sin brought sickness and death into the world. And my own sins deserve more pains than I can have to bear. I complain not against Thee, but against myself.

O LORD, I am sick! So Thy best saints have been—Job, Hezekiah, Lazarus, Dorcas. What then do I, a sinner, deserve? But, LORD, forsake me not.

O LORD, I am sick! and sickness is a warning of death. All must die once, and I among the rest. If now I die in Thy favour, Thy will be done; let it be even now. But let me not live to lose Thy favour, nor die in Thy displeasure. Whether I live or die, let me be Thine.

O LORD, I am sick! But Thou canst make we well. Thy Hand heals all: Thy Word can rebuke my sickness. Let Thy Hand be laid upon me, and Thy Blessing be given to me. Speak the word only, and Thy servant shall be whole. LORD, I believe Thy power; I pray for Thy help. Let me lie still, O LORD, under Thy Hand in hope; and with patience wait Thy Word.

O LORD, I am sick! So I have been before, and Thou hast made me well. Death might have come; but Thou saidst the word, and I lived. And Thou canst do the same again. LORD, if Thou wilt, Thou canst; and Thou art merciful.

O LORD, I am sick! But Thou wilt some day make me well, if I will—like an angel of heaven that is never sick. O let me never be so fond of earth as to give up the hope of heaven; nor so love to live with men, as to loathe to die and be like unto the angels.

O LORD, I am sick! But that may make we well. Shew me my sins. Quicken my repentance, increase my sorrow, exercise my patience. Make my heart dead to this world: raise up my soul, and prepare it for a better life. Make my malady thus to be my medicine, by Thy grace, O LORD; and then even in health I shall not do so well.

O LORD, I am sick! Sick in body, let my heart be sound —in Thy truth, that I be not led astray—in Thy fear, that I be not tempted beyond my strength—in Thy peace, that I be not troubled beyond measure. Let neither man nor devil, flesh nor world delude and destroy me. May GOD, make and keep me thus sound.

O LORD, I am sick and in pain! But, O my dear Saviour, what is my bed to Thy Cross? What is my bitterness to Thy cup? What are my groans to Thy cries? What are the restless thoughts of my head to Thy sharp crown of thorns? What is my agony to Thy bloody sweat? What are my faintings to Thy wounds? What are my pains to Thy Passion? O let me see Thee on Thy Cross, that I may suffer all my pain with patience.

O LORD, I am sick! So are many thousands more as much as I, and thousands worse than I. And were my sickness the worst,—What is the pain of my body to the sin of my soul? What is my bed to hell? What is my woe to the worm? What is my malady to the fire? What is all my light and short affliction to that infinite and eternal pain? O LORD, how great is Thy mercy! Show Thy mercy upon me, and grant me Thy salvation?

And now, LORD, I lay down my life at Thy feet; I leave my soul in Thy hands. O GOD, look upon me. Take care of me. Appoint Thy angels my keepers. Be Thyself my Physician, and the Precious Blood my remedy. Let Thy providence watch with me; Thy mercy make my bed in my sickness; Thy peace lay the pillow under my head. Let the visitation of the Blessed Spirit refresh my soul, and defend me from the spirits of darkness. Under Thy wings, O LORD, is my refuge, and into Thy arms I cast myself. Hold me, keep me, comfort me. Let Thy wings be over me, and Thine arms embrace me, O GOD of my life and my hope. So let me lie down, and sleep, and take my rest.

105.—HYMNS.

My soul and body faint with pain,
  And life is sad to me;
But, Father, I would not complain,
  For all is known to Thee.

Thou seest every grief and care,
  Thou hearest every sigh;
Thou knowest all I have to bear,
  How feeble, too, am I.

'Tis hard to calm my troubled heart,
  'Tis hard to kiss the rod;
'Tis hard to feel that still Thou art
  My Father and my GOD.

My faith is weak; O make me know,
  While here I helpless lie,
And wonder why I suffer so,
  That, LORD, Thou knowest why.

'Tis not for me to fly from care,
  I would not sorrow shun;
Be this my quiet, humble prayer—
  Father, Thy will be done.

For Thou art Love, Thou lovest me,
  And Thou art Wisdom too;
And sorrow does not work for Thee
  What happiness could do.

I should not have to bear my pain,
  And grieve so many days,
If what I need my soul could gain
  By easy, pleasant ways.

So may I rest, content that now
  Through grief Thy love should bless;
And long to be with those whom Thou
  Dost train by happiness.

When I am ready, bring me where
  There is no grief to shun,
Where life is all one joyous prayer—
  "Father, Thy will be done."
                T. B. P.

Jesu, lover of my soul,
  Let me to Thy bosom fly,
While the nearer waters roll,
  While the tempest still is high!
Hide me, O my Saviour, hide,
  Till the storm of life is past,
Safe into the haven guide;
  O receive my soul at last!

Other refuge have I none,
  Hangs my helpless soul on Thee;
Leave, ah! leave me not alone,
  Still support and comfort me!
All my trust on Thee is stayed,
  All my help from Thee I bring,
Cover my defenceless head
  With the shadow of Thy wing!

Wilt Thou not regard my call?
  Wilt Thou not accept my prayer?
Lo! I sink, I faint, I fall!
  Lo! on Thee I cast my care!
Reach me out Thy gracious hand!
  While I of Thy strength receive,
Hoping against hope I stand:
  Dying, and behold I live!

Thou, O Christ, art all I want;
  More than all in Thee I find:
Raise the fallen, cheer the faint,
  Heal the sick, and lead the blind!
Just and Holy is Thy Name;
  I am all unrighteousness;
False and full of sin I am,
  Thou art full of truth and grace.

Plenteous grace with Thee is found,
  Grace to cover all my sin;
Let the healing streams abound,
  Make and keep me pure within!
Thou of Life the fountain art,
  Freely let me take of Thee;
Spring Thou up within my heart,
  Rise to all eternity!

Rock of Ages, cleft for me,
Let me hide myself in Thee!
Let the water and the blood,
From Thy riven Side which flowed,
Be of sin the double cure,
Cleanse me from its guilt and power.

Not the labours of my hands
Can fulfil Thy law's demands;
Could my zeal no respite know,

Could my tears for ever flow,
All for sin could not atone;
Thou must save, and Thou alone.

Nothing in my hand I bring;
Simply to Thy Cross I cling;
Naked, come to Thee for dress;
Helpless, look to Thee for grace;
Foul, I to the Fountain fly:
Wash me Saviour, or I die.

While I draw this fleeting breath,
When mine eyes are closed in death,
When I soar through worlds unknown,
See Thee on Thy judgment throne;
Rock of Ages, cleft for me,
Let me hide myself in Thee.

———

Father, if Thou willing be,
  Then my griefs a while suspend;
Then remove the cup from me,
  Or Thy strengthening angel send:
Wouldest Thou have me suffer on?
Father, let Thy will be done.

Let my flesh be troubled still,
  Filled with pain or sore disease;
Let my wounded spirit feel
  Strong, redoubled agonies;
Meekly I my will resign
Thine be done and only Thine.

Patient as my great High-Priest,
  In His bitterness of pain;
Most abandoned and distressed,
  Father, I the cross sustain:
All into Thy hands I give,
Let me die or let me live.

Following where my LORD hath led,
  Thee I on the cross adore,
Humbly bow like Him my head,
  All Thy benefits restore,
Till my spirit I resign,
Breathed into the hands divine.

———

Now it belongs not to my care
  Whether I die or live;
To love and serve Thee is my share,
  And this Thy grace must give.

Come, LORD, when grace hath made me meet
  Thy blessed face to see:
For, if Thy work on earth be sweet,
  What must Thy glory be?

Then I shall end my sad complaints,
  And weary, sinful days;
And join with the triumphant saints
  That sing Jehovah's praise.

My knowledge of that life is small,
  The eye of faith is dim;
But it's enough that CHRIST knows all,
  And I shall be with Him.

———

When languor and disease invade
  This trembling house of clay;
'Tis sweet to look beyond our cage,
  And long to fly away.

Sweet to look inward, and attend
  The whispers of His love;
Sweet to look upward to the place,
  Where JESUS pleads above.

Sweet to look back and see my name
  In life's fair book set down:
Sweet to look forward, and behold
  Eternal joys my own.

Sweet on His faithfulness to rest,
  Whose love can never end:
Sweet on His covenant of grace
  For all things to depend.

Sweet to rejoice in lively hope,
  That, when my change shall come,
Angels will hover round my bed,
  And waft my spirit home.

If such the views which grace unfolds,
  Weak as it is below;
What raptures must the Church above
  In JESUS' Presence know!

If such the sweetness of the stream,
  What must the fountain be,
Where Saints and Angels draw their bliss
  Immediately from Thee.
[*See Chapter* 100.]

106.—RECOVERY FROM SICKNESS.

Glory be to Thee, O Heavenly Father. The stripes Thou didst lay upon me were stripes of love.

In mercy didst Thou send me this sickness. Before I was troubled I went wrong, but now will I keep Thy Word.

It is good for me that I have been in trouble, that I might learn Thy statutes.

I called upon the LORD in my trouble, and the LORD heard me. I shall not die but live, and declare the works of the LORD.

Praise the LORD, O my soul, and all that is within me praise His Holy Name; Who hath saved Thy life from destruction, and crowned thee with mercy and loving-kindness.

O LORD, my GOD, I cried unto Thee, and Thou hast healed me; therefore will I sing of Thy praise without ceasing.

LORD, I desire to pay Thee my vows which I promised when I was in trouble. Give me a heart always ready to perform all my good resolutions. Help me to show my thankfulness, not only by words, but also by my life.

I was smitten, LORD; but Thou hast healed me. The blow was just: Thy help is gracious. My sins deserved death: Thy mercy has given me life.

And now, LORD, let my heart smite me; because I rebelled against Thee and Thy goodness to me: let Thy grace keep me, that I may always obey Thee. Let not the sickness go from my body to my soul. Let not sin and Satan destroy me. Let not others be infected with evil by me, lest a worse thing come unto me.

Ever-blessed be Thy Name! May I never dishonour it again! May I ever honour it, and praise Thee more and more. Amen.

107.—THOUGHTS ON RECOVERY.

I am recovered, O LORD! Whoever was the doctor, Thou art the GOD of my health. Whatever was the medicine, Thine was the remedy. Whoever took care of me, Thou didst work the cure for me. So let me regard the physician as the instrument of my healing, Thee as the author — medicines as the means, Thee as their maker—friends as my helpers, Thee as my keeper. Let me give their due thanks to them, and Thy due glory to Thee.

I am recovered, O LORD! out of many thousands at the same time sick, how many are dead! Of those that suffered from the same disease as I, how many are buried! And many of them were of better life before Thee than I have been, and were of greater use to the Church and the world than I can be. Make me feel this Thy great goodness and mercy, O LORD; and, while my breath lasts, may I be thankful for my life.

I am recovered, O LORD! And yet, when my day and my hour come, I must die. Far off the time cannot be: Thou knowest how soon it will come. My life is held at Thy will: my health is more uncertain than my life. Whilst I have life and health, let me not misspend the minutes of remaining time on vile or vain things or ends; but redeem what has been lost in lust, to use to Thy honour and my happiness; by securing the full possession of that blessed eternity, for which I have and hold my short lease of life and time.

I am recovered, O LORD! Not to sin against Thee, but to serve Thee. Let me not sin more, because I live more; lest a worse thing befall me—some grievous disease of body, or more fearful sickness of soul—a body sick, or heart hard, even unto death. If, when Thou lookest for an amendment of life with my health, I use my health to return to sin and folly,—what hope of life then for soul or body? For that wrong done to Thy mercy, what can I look for from Thy justice, but that, since my sick bed has made me no better, death will make my next bed, and vengeance will lay me in that fatal sleep from which I shall have no hope of waking?

I am recovered, O LORD! Thou hast given me what I wished, my health: let me give me what Thou willest, Thy service. I owe it ever to Thee; for it is due to Thy command, to Thy preservation of my life, and to my promise. Let me pay at least once what I owe thrice; lest I bring on myself a three-fold penalty for being undutiful, unthankful, and unfaithful. What I would be in sickness, let me be in health; and in the state I desired to die, let it be my care to live; lest, when death comes, my spirit be not revived by the comfort of a good life;—lest my heart be vexed by the remembrance of hypocrisy or apostacy;—lest, for being false in sickness or foul in health, Thou deny all hope to my dying soul; and just horror seize me for being untrue to Thy laws, Thy mercies, and my promises.

I am recovered, O LORD! And from falling to my grave, am raised off my bed. Let me look at my life as a resurrection from the dead, and an exchange of a dying for a living life. And, as Thou hast granted me two lives on earth, let me once for all give myself to Thee as Thy servant. Let me dedicate the new life, now given, to Thy fear; and, if for years past the old life has been too little devoted to Thee, let me be the more careful for the future to keep holy the dedication of the new.

I am recovered, O LORD! In body; but let me be so in soul. Let me pray and try to the utmost that I may be: let me see and know why I should be. Let me value the health of my body as a jewel of comfort, but the health of my soul as a crown of rejoicing: for my body is but the casket, and my soul is the treasure. With my health then I beg Thy grace, O GOD; that I may have a sound soul in a sound body. LORD, perfect Thy cure. Heal me not half but whole. Give me as much conscience to seek the one as I have sense to find the other; lest, when I have my body sound and leave my soul sick, both soul and body at last die for ever of that sickness. Sanctify my sickness past to be my safeguard against the plague of sin, and my body's health to be my soul's hope.

I am recovered, O LORD! And I have found out too, how

unfit a season, a sick time; how unfit a place, a sick bed; how unfit a person one who is sick is, to work out that good and great work of Thy service and the sinner's salvation. I have learned how hard it is for me to think at once of body and soul, of earth and heaven — to consider my ways in the confusion of my thoughts. I know that, when head is disturbed, heart oppressed, spirit broken,—when all the powers of my mind are weakened, and all the limbs of my body helpless, and when all my strength is departed—I know that then I cannot love and serve the LORD with all my heart, with all my soul, with all my mind, and with all my strength. When all the advantages which flesh and blood can give are against me, and are on the side of my soul's enemy —how, then, can I fight him for a crown? What hope is there for me, when I can better roar in the disquietness of my heart, than cry in the fervency of my spirit; and when, for rejecting the offers and succours of grace in health, I may justly fear that GOD will rather forsake me than assist me, and rather give me up than defend me, in my sickness? What can I do, when death and wrath at once affright me, and the knowledge of all my sin tempts me to despair?—when I cannot repent for want of power —when I have no memory, no mind, no will for such a work; and no mouth, no eyes, no knees for such holy business—when, if I had power to repent, I cannot amend for want of time—when my soul is readier to depart from the world of sin than from the sins of the world, and my body is in a state more fit to trouble than to help my soul? How should I turn my heart within me, that cannot turn myself on my bed? How can I lift up my heart, when I can scarce raise my head? LORD, by the experience I have now had in sickness, let me learn the need and the wisdom,— whilst I am in health and strength, and vigour of life and spirit,—of undertaking and overcoming the high, holy, hard, and only needful business of preparation for heaven.

I am recovered, O LORD! But how many at this hour lie sick as I was, and even worse than I have been—torn, racked, wasted with disease and pain! O let not pity leave my heart, as pain leaves my body. Let me not deny them what prayer or help, what heart or hand can do. And, O GOD of mercy, Who hast both hand and heart, both power and love to help: be Physician and Comforter to them all. Help them, Good LORD, to patience, hope, physicians for soul and body, comfort, friends, counsels, medicines, food—all things needful for saving of soul, support of life, recovery of health, and a happy issue of all their afflictions.

I am recovered, O LORD! But what is my health to that of heaven, where soul is without danger of sin, body without danger of sickness, mind without error, will without lust, memory without fail, conscience without guilt— where the soul, alive unto GOD and united to GOD, is strong in all the powers of healthy and happy life for ever!—where the body shall not need to feed or sleep; nor fear to be diseased or deformed; nor complain of disorder or accident; nor suffer death or decay; but be cleansed and glorified to take part in GOD'S high worship, and enjoy man's eternal bliss.

O let me neglect no earthly medicines to procure myself that heavenly health. Let the Church be my home, the Bible my garden, meditation my walk, private devotion my retirement, prayer my breath, repentance my labour, fasting my food, alms my exercise, affliction my bread, tears my wine, the Eucharist my feast, the saints my music, angels my keepers, divines my fathers, Thy peace my rest. Let me make a prison my house, a rack my bed, and chains my ornaments; may I water my bed with my tears, and lie in a bath of my blood; may I do all that Saints did, and suffer all that Confessors did in life or Martyrs did unto death, rather than lose or pass by a remedy needful for the health of my soul.

And when I have done and borne all, let Thy Blood, O JESU, purge me that I be not foul; and may the Holy Spirit be my Comforter, that I do not faint. May the Truth always be my prescription, that I may not err. So let my body's health on earth, whet a holy appetite and hunger in my soul; and all my longings of soul and body be only satisfied at the Marriage Supper of the Lamb in heaven.

I am recovered, O LORD! How happy, as well as healthy, shall I be, if I recover all this good by my recovery!—if, by Thy rich grace, I be for the future more hopeful in Providence, more thankful for life, more mindful of death, more fearful of sin, more dutiful in service, more careful of soul, more watchful of time, more sorry for the afflicted on earth, more joyful in the hope of heaven.

O LORD GOD of my health and salvation, Who hast given Thy servant a present health of body after his sickness: Receive the thanks which I offer, and bless the resolutions which I make, and hearken to the prayers which I pray before Thee; that, when the sickness comes which will be my death, Thou mayest give me a recovery of that Paradise which by man's sin was lost, and the loss of which brought in sickness and death upon us all—even a place in that higher and better Paradise, where no sin or sorrow, pain or death can ever come.

Grant this for Thine infinite mercies' sake, O LORD GOD, Father of heaven, the great helper and healer of all our infirmities.

Grant it for Thine infinite mercies' sake, LORD JESUS, Son of the Father, Whose Precious Blood heals all souls, Who art indeed the Saviour of the world.

Grant it for Thine infinite mercies' sake, Holy and Eternal Spirit, Who by Thy seven-fold gifts of grace healeth our sickness and helpeth our infirmities.

Father, Son, and Holy Ghost; grant me this full and final recovery of soul and body, now and for ever. Amen.

108.—FOR ONE WHO IS DEPARTING.

Into Thy merciful hands, O LORD, we commend the soul of Thy servant. Acknowledge, we beseech Thee, a work of Thine own hands, a sheep of Thine own fold, a lamb of Thine own flock, a sinner of Thine own redeeming. Receive *him* into the blessed arms of Thine unspeakable mercy, into the sacred rest of everlasting peace, and into the glorious estate of Thy chosen saints in heaven. *Amen.*

GOD the Father, Who hath created Thee; GOD the Son, Who hath redeemed thee; GOD the Holy Ghost, Who hath poured His grace into thee, be now and evermore thy defence, assist thee in thy last trial, and bring thee to everlasting life. *Amen*

JESUS CHRIST, that redeemed thee with his agony and bloody Death, have mercy upon thee, and strengthen thee in thy last agony. *Amen.*

JESUS CHRIST, that rose on the third day from death, raise thee up in the resurrection of the just. *Amen.*

JESUS CHRIST, that ascended into heaven, and now sitteth at the right hand of the Father, bring thee into the place of eternal happiness and joy. *Amen.*

GOD the Father preserve and keep thee. GOD the Son assist and strengthen thee. GOD the Holy Ghost comfort and defend thee. GOD the Holy Trinity, LORD of heaven and earth, be ever with thee, hearken into the prayers of His Church in heaven and earth, drive away from thee all the hosts of Satan, and give the Holy Angels charge concerning thee. *Amen.*

Lord now lettest Thou Thy servant depart in peace.

Into thy hands, O LORD, we commend *his* spirit; for Thou hast redeemed *him*, O LORD, Thou GOD of truth.

Say unto *his* soul, I am thy salvation.

Say unto *him*, This day shalt thou be with Me in Paradise.

Let *him* now feel the salvation of JESUS.

Let *him* now feel the anointing of CHRIST.

Guide *him* through the valley of the shadow of death.

Let *him* see the goodness of the LORD in the land of the living.

O LORD, command *his* spirit to be received up to Thee in peace.

O LORD, bid *him* to come to Thee over the water.

LORD JESUS, receive *his* spirit.

Open to *him* the gates of everlasting glory.

Send Thine angels to meet *him*.

Let Thy good Spirit lead *him* into the land of righteousness.

Bring *him* to Thy holy hill and to Thy dwelling.

Place *him* in the abode of light and peace, of joy and gladness.

Receive *him* in the arms of Thy mercy.

Give *him* an inheritance with the Saints in Light.

109.—THE DEPARTED.
Office for the Departed.

In the Name of the ✠ Father, and of the Son, and of the Holy Ghost. *Amen.*

When our heads are bowed with woe,
When our bitter tears o'erflow,
When we mourn the lost, the dear,
JESU, Son of Mary, hear.

Psalm 130.
1 *Thess.* iv. 13-18.

Our Father.

Everlasting rest, LORD, give to them: *And perpetual light shine upon them.*

I believe that I shall see the goodness of the Lord: *In the land of the living.*

May they rest in peace. *Amen.*

LORD, incline Thine ear unto our prayers, wherein we devoutly call upon Thy mercy to bestow the souls of Thy servants, both men and women, that Thou hast called away from this world, in the country of peace and rest; and cause them to be made partakers with thy Saints; through CHRIST our LORD. *Amen.*

God have mercy on all Christian souls. *Amen.*

For one Departed.

Almighty and Eternal GOD, to whom no prayer is ever made without hope of mercy: Be gracious to the soul of Thy servant; that, as it departed this life in the confession of Thy Name, Thou mayest cause it to be joined to the company of Thy Saints. *Amen.*

For Father and Mother Departed.

O LORD, who hast commanded me to honour my father and mother: Have mercy on the souls of my father and my mother, take away all the stains of their sins, and grant me to live with them in bliss without end. *Amen.*

For those who Departed this Day.

O GOD, to whom only it belongeth ever to have mercy and to spare: We make our prayer unto Thee for the souls of all men and women, Thy servants, whom Thou hast this day called out of this world. Give them not into the hands of the enemy, neither forget them at the last. Command them to be taken up by Holy Angels and led into the kingdom of life; and, as they hoped and believed in Thee, make them ever to be glad in the company of Thy Saints. *Amen.*

Anniversaries.

LORD GOD of mercy: Grant to the souls of Thy servants, whom we remember this day, a place of refreshment, happy rest, and clear light. *Amen.*

Souls not Remembered.

LORD GOD, we pray Thee, through the precious Passion of Thy only-begotten Son our LORD JESUS CHRIST, to have mercy on all departed souls, that have none to bring the remembrance of them before Thee. They are formed in Thine image and are signed with the sign of faith. Spare them, and preserve those whom Thou hast made. Despise not the work of Thine own hands. Stretch forth Thy right hand over them, give them hope and comfort, and join them to the company of Thy Saints; through Thine exceeding great mercy in JESUS CHRIST our LORD. *Amen.*

In a Churchyard.

Health and safety to all faithful souls, whose bodies rest in the dust, here and in all places! May our LORD JESUS CHRIST, Who redeemed them with His own most Precious Blood, vouchsafe to keep them from all evil, and join them to the company of the angels! And may the Heavenly Host assist us with their prayers; that, by the mercy of GOD, we may have fellowship with them, and be crowned with them in the kingdom of our LORD JESUS CHRIST. *Amen.*

110.—EPITAPHS.

In peace.
In CHRIST.
Sleeping in JESUS.
May *he* rest in peace.
Blessed are the dead which die in the LORD.
Blessed be the Name of the LORD.
The LORD gave, and the LORD hath taken away.
Thy will be done.
It is well with the child.
O Lamb of GOD, That takest away the sin of the world, grant *him* Thy peace.
JESU mercy!
GOD be merciful to me a sinner.
The LORD grant unto *him* that *he* may find mercy of the LORD in that day.
LORD, have mercy upon *him.*
Spare *him* good LORD.
Good LORD deliver *him.*
In the Day of Judgment, good LORD deliver *him.*
By Thy Precious Death and Burial good LORD deliver *him.*
Pray for us.
Pray for me.
Pray for the soul of —— —— who departed —— ——
[" *departed* " *is better than* " *died* " *or* " *deceased.*"]

Through your prayers I shall be given unto you.
Enter not into judgment with Thy servant, O LORD.
GOD have mercy on all Christian souls.
LORD JESUS, receive my spirit.
Into Thy hands I commend my spirit.
The LORD JESUS CHRIST be with thy spirit.
Absent from the body. Present with the LORD.
Neither death nor life shall be able to separate us from the love of GOD.
He is able to keep that which I have committed unto Him against that day.
She is not dead but sleepeth.
So He giveth His beloved sleep.
Them which sleep in JESUS will GOD bring with Him.
Thy *brother* shall rise again.
I know that *he* shall rise again.
I know that my Redeemer liveth.
I will walk before the LORD in the land of the living.
Thou shalt show me the path of life.
Weep not.
Weep not for me.
Rejoice with me.
Comfort one another.
GOD shall wipe away all tears from their eyes.
Come, LORD JESUS.
LORD come and see.
Waiting for the coming of

our LORD JESUS CHRIST.

Looking for that blessed hope.

In hope of Eternal Life.

By Thy glorious Resurrection, good LORD deliver me.

He Which raised up the LORD JESUS, shall raise up us also by JESUS, and shall present us with you.

Thanks be to GOD Which giveth us the victory.

LORD, remember me when Thou comest into Thy kingdom.

Thou art with me.

Make *him* to be numbered with Thy Saints in glory everlasting.

Everlasting rest, LORD, give to *him;* and perpetual light shine upon *him.*

There remaineth a rest to the people of GOD.

LORD, all-pitying JESU blest
Grant *him* Thine Eternal Rest.
LORD, Who didst *his* soul redeem,
Grant a blessed Requiem.

Grant *him* Thine Eternal Rest
With the Spirits of the Blest.

Come that day, when I shall never
Sleep again, but Wake for ever.

111.—IN ALL CHANGES.

O Almighty GOD, Who alone canst order the unruly wills and affections of sinful men: Grant unto Thy people, that they may love the thing which Thou commandest, and desire that which Thou dost promise; that so, among the sundry and manifold changes of the world, our hearts may surely there be fixed, where true joys are to be found; through JESUS CHRIST our LORD. *Amen.*

PART VIII.—THE SEASONS OF THE CHURCH.

"My people shall dwell in a peaceable habitation, and in sure dwellings, and in quiet Resting-places."—*Isaiah* xxxii. 18.

112.—DIVISIONS OF TIME.

Chapters 113-118 are not added to Part VII.; for the divisions of time are not among the varying changes of the world, but are *fixed* arrangements of GOD's providence. Those Chapters are placed in Part VIII.; for every year is a year "of our LORD," and its divisions mark the duration of Church Seasons.

Chapters 119-141 concern in the first place the Seasons of the Church; but some of them, in their turn, are used by the world in its reckoning of time.

113.—THE YEAR.

GOD of my life, Who hast given me [this day] to see a new year begun: Give me grace to lead a new life to the end of all my years. Give me a new heart, that I may always walk in truth before Thee, have Thy peace within me, and rejoice in Thy blessing upon me; for His sake Who was content to be born at this time, and [on this day] to be circumcised and to be called JESUS. Amen.

Time himself, with all his legions,
Days, Months, Years, since nature's birth,
Shall revive,—and from all regions
Singling out the sons of earth,
With their glory or disgrace,
Charge their spenders face to face.

Every moment of my being
Then shall pass before mine eyes:
GOD, all searching! GOD, all seeing!
Oh! appease them, ere they rise:
Warned I fly, I fly to Thee:
GOD, be merciful to me!
See Chapter 122.]

114.—FOUR SEASONS OF THE YEAR.

[*The order of these prayers, when said together, is—Winter, Spring, Summer, Autumn. Compare S. Matt.* xiii. 1—23. *S. Mark* iv. 1—20. *S. Luke* viii. 5—15.]

Spring.

LORD JESUS, help me with joy and without delay to receive into my heart the seed of Thy Holy Word. Let not that precious seed be lost. Water it by the continual dew of Thy blessing; that I may be rooted in Thee, and grow up into Thee. Let not the sun nor any heat scorch me; May no trouble or persecution cause my leaf to wither. May I never be offended because of Thy Word. Confirm the babes of Thy flock; that, desiring the sincere milk of the Word, they may grow thereby. Amen.

Summer.

LORD JESUS, help me to grow in grace and in the knowledge of Thee. Save me from the cares of the world, and the desire of riches, and the lusts of other things. Suffer me not to go forth rashly unto them; and suffer them not to enter violently into me; lest the plant, which has grown up, be choked with thorns, and become unfruitful. Save the young men and the young women who are strong; and suffer not any evil to overcome them. May the leaves of profession and the flowers of promise bring forth, in their season, the fruit of good works, to the glory of Thy Name. Amen.

Autumn.

LORD JESUS, create in me a clean heart, and renew a right spirit within me. May the good seed be received into an honest and good heart: may it spring up, and increase, and bear abundant fruit. Help me to go on with patience, and, through Thy great mercy alone, lay up goods for many years, even for ever and ever. Keep Thy people firm unto the end. Ripen the graces of those of riper years. May the fathers, who have known Thee long, be constant to the end. And while good and bad grow together now in Thy field, save the good from the evil, and save the evil by changing them into good. Turn the hearts of the disobedient to the wisdom of the just. Gather in both bad and good, that Thy garners may be plenteous with all manner of store. Send forth labourers into Thy field now, that Thy angels may fill Thy barns in the end. Amen.

Winter.

LORD JESUS, deliver me from hardness of heart; that I may hide within my heart the seed that is sown there; and guard it reverently, lest it be trodden under foot of men. Give me understanding, that I may keep Thy word; and may so keep myself, that that wicked one touch me not. Prosper all the work of Thy Church; that

the seed may be sown in the whole field of the world; and that even the wayfaring man may hear the Gospel, and may not neglect so great salvation. Drive away the fowls of the air; that they may neither catch away and devour the small seed, when they light upon the ground; nor destroy the fruit, when they lodge among the branches of the great tree. Amen.
[*See Chapter* 118.]

115.—THE MONTH.
For Stedfastness.

O Sun of Righteousness, Whose light is always pure and perfect, Whose Face never changes nor deceives: Look with mercy on us sinners, who desire to shine with Thy light, and to be perfect as Thou art perfect. While some lights wane and die, let Thy Light in us wax brighter and brighter unto the perfect day—the day of Thy appearing and Thy glory.

In Faith.

O GOD, Who wilt not suffer us to be tempted above what we are able to bear: Come to my relief, and keep me stedfast in the faith. Teach me so much of the ways of Thy Providence that I may see why I should never doubt or deny it. And since Thy ways are past finding out, help me to adore the wisdom and the justice which I cannot understand. Let no trial tempt me to forsake Thee, to deny Thy works, or to reject Thy Gospel; for JESUS CHRIST'S sake. Amen.

In Duty.

O GOD, Who art always true and good: Make me constant in holding the truth and striving after goodness. Let me not give up the true faith, nor despair of living a good life. Help me to see others go back from Thee, and not follow them. Help me to hear of new things, and not heed them. O LORD JESUS CHRIST, Who art yesterday, to-day, and for ever, the same: Give me the help of the Holy Ghost, that I may be to-day what I was yesterday in all good things; and that I may not lose to-morrow any good that I have to-day. Make me always to be what I ought to be, always the same, always growing in grace, Thine for ever and ever. Amen.

In Faith and Duty.

O merciful GOD, Who hast granted me so many favours: Add this also, I beseech Thee, that I may keep the right faith in all humility, and have perfect charity with all men; that I may seriously endeavour to serve Thee my LORD with a pure heart and a chaste body, even to my life's end;

and, after all my labours, may enter into Thine eternal joy. Amen.

116.—THE WEEK.
Genesis I.

Come, Holy Ghost, renew the face
Of all the earth; and drive
The old man from us by Thy grace;
To make the new man thrive.

O GOD, MY CREATOR,

1. Cause the light to shine out of darkness. Shine in my heart. Send out Thy light and Thy truth, that they may lead me, and bring me unto Thy holy hill and to Thy dwelling. Amen.

2. Divide the waters from the waters. Give me true repentance,—not the sorrow of the world, but godly sorrow that worketh repentance unto salvation. Let me, by Thy mercy, be drawn out of the water and become Thy true disciple. Amen.

3. Make dry land to appear and make it fruitful too. Dry up my tears of penitence, and give me firm ground of comfort in Thy Word. May I bring forth good fruit here, and may I hereafter eat of the tree of life in the midst of the Paradise of GOD. Amen.

4. May the Sun of Righteousness shine upon my soul, drawing away from it all damp mists of ignorance and folly, softening my cold frozen heart, teaching me daily to follow Him as He runs His course, guiding me in the darkness of this world by the moon that receives His light; till at last the Moon's light is as the light of the Sun, and the Church is like her LORD, and the righteous shine as the Sun in the kingdom of their Father. Amen.

5. May the Blessed Spirit move upon the waters of the rain from heaven, and make them fruitful. Let not the waters of the earth prevail: let not those things which I have wrought be lost in the water-flood of despair. Let not the fowls of the air devour my fruit: let not the evil spirits take Thy Word out of my heart. Give me the wings of a dove: may the Spirit, Who descended like a dove, raise me on silver wings to my holy Resting-place of peace and joy. Amen.

6. Let it never be in the power of any creature, in heaven or earth, to mar Thy best works again. And though I have sinned and made myself like unto the beasts that perish, be pleased to renew me after Thine own image. Thy hands have made me and fashioned me: O give me understanding, that I may learn Thy commandments, and may wear a crown of glory in Thy heavenly kingdom. Amen.

7. Grant unto me, after the painful labours of this life are ended, a sweet, blessed, and everlasting rest with Thee. May this hope so comfort my heart, that I may not fail in my labours, nor faint in my wanderings, nor sink under my burdens, nor fall under my crosses, nor die of my wounds; but go on cheerfully and bravely to the Eden above. Amen.

[*See Parts V., VI.*]

117.—THE DAY.

O GOD, into the hands of Thy mercy and lovingkindness I humbly commend my soul and my body, my mind and my thoughts, my words and my deeds, my devotions and my work, [my father and my mother, my brothers and my sisters,] my friends and my relations; that thou mayest keep me and mine, by day and by night, every hour and every moment; beseeching on our behalf Thy most loving mercy, that Thou wouldest grant unto us sinners pardon of our sins, escape and deliverance from present ills, security and caution as to the future, strong perseverance in Thy Faith, and a devout will to do our duty; in all our prosperity in this world, wisdom and humility; in the good things of Thy grace, abundance of all spiritual gifts, charity and perfect patience. Grant to our friends and benefactors, mercy and everlasting glory; to our enemies contrition and pardon. To all grant space for true repentance and amendment of life; the grace and consolation of the Holy Spirit, and perseverance in good works; all things profitable for the safety of the body and the salvation of the soul; grace and holy living here, glory and endless life hereafter. Amen.

[*See Part IV.*]

118.—HARVEST.

O Almighty and everlasting GOD, Who hast given unto us the fruits of the earth in their season: Grant us grace to use the same to Thy glory, the relief of those that need, and our own comfort, through JESUS CHRIST, Who is the Living Bread, Which cometh down from heaven and giveth life unto the world; to Whom, with Thee and the Holy Ghost, be all honour and glory, world without end. *Amen.*

O LORD, we pray Thee, sow the seed of Thy Word in our hearts, and send down upon us Thy heavenly grace; that we may bring forth the fruits of the Spirit, and at the Great Day may be gathered by Thy holy angels into Thy garner, through JESUS CHRIST our LORD. *Amen.*

[*See Chapter 114.*]

119.—ADVENT.

O GOD, by Whose providence Thy Church hath appointed the solemn time of Advent to come before the celebration of our Saviour's birth, and prepare its way in our hearts: Grant me so to employ this holy season, that my heart may be raised to celebrate the feast of Christmas with great joy, and be able to look and wait for the second coming of our LORD JESUS CHRIST, Who, with Thee and the Holy Ghost, liveth and reigneth, one GOD, world without end. Amen.

I believe, O blessed JESUS, that, from Thy throne at the right hand of the Father, Thou wilt come again to judge the world. O let the last trumpet be ever sounding in my ears, that I may always be mindful of the account that I have to give; and may not think or speak or do anything that may wound my own conscience, provoke Thy anger, or cause me to tremble at that awful day.

JESU, Who our Judge art coming,
Saints rewarding, sinners dooming,
Gracious Saviour, righteous LORD!
In Thy loving mercy chide me
Ere I call the rocks to hide me
Outcast from Thy Face abhorred.

Four Last Things.

Death.

LORD JESUS, teach me so to live, that, when I die, I may come to a better life. Help me daily to repent of daily sins. Living or dying may I be Thine. Save me from an unprepared heart and an unexpected end. Amen.

Judgment.

LORD JESUS, make me to judge myself daily, that I be not condemned at the last day. Let me fall down humbly before the throne of Thy mercy, that I may be able to stand before the throne of Thy justice, and may for ever dwell in the home of Thy love. Amen.

Hell.

LORD JESUS, from Thy throne in heaven look upon the earth Thy footstool, and cast me not into Thy prison of hell. Make me often think of hell, that I may never come to it, or indulge any sin that may lead me to it. O suffer me not to buy any sin so dearly as to lose heaven for it, and go to hell because of it. Be not angry with me for ever. Save me, good LORD, by the merits of Thy Precious Blood and Passion. Amen.

Heaven.

LORD JESUS, Who hast bought heaven for me by Thy Blood, and now keepest it for me in Thy Body: Fill my soul with the inspirations of Thy Holy Spirit, that my life on earth may be heavenly, and that my portion for ever may be in heaven. O let me not, for the short pleasures of this life, lose the joy of Thy Presence in Thy kingdom. Thou hast prepared heaven for Thy saints: preserve me for heaven, and make me to be numbered with Thy saints. Amen.

Litany.
Jesu, Life of those who die,
Advocate with God on high,
Hope of Immortality,
 Hear us, Holy Jesu!

Death.
Thou, Whose death to mortals gave
Power to triumph o'er the grave;
Living now from death to save,
 Hear us, Holy Jesu!

Judgment.
Thou, before Whose great white Throne,
All our evil must be shewn;
Pleading now for us Thine own,
 Hear us, Holy Jesu!

Hell.
Thou, Whose death was borne that we,
From the power of Satan free,
Might not die eternally,
 Hear us, Holy Jesu!

Heaven.
Thou, Who dost a place prepare,
That in heavenly mansions fair,
Sinners may Thy glory share,
 Hear us, Holy Jesu!
  Amen.
  T. B. P.

120.—EMBER DAYS IN ADVENT.
[*See Chapters* 127, 144-149, 114 *Winter.*]

121.—CHRISTMAS.
O God, Who makest us glad with the yearly remembrance of the birth of Thine only Son Jesus Christ: Grant that, as we joyfully receive Him as our Redeemer, so we may with sure confidence behold Him, when He shall come to be our Judge; Who liveth and reigneth with Thee and the Holy Ghost, one God, world without end. *Amen.*

Gracious Lord Jesus Christ, Son of God, Saviour of men, Joy of angels, Dread of devils; the Jews' Messiah, and the Gentiles' Star; the Hope of the living, and the Resurrection of the dead; the Way to all that come to Thee, the Truth to all that know Thee, and the Life to all that believe in Thee: Make good all Thy glorious titles unto me. Lord protect me. Jesus save me; Christ, my anointed king, rule me; my anointed priest sanctify me; my anointed prophet teach me, and reveal to me the secrets of Thy kingdom.

This is the day which the LORD hath made: I will rejoice and be glad in it. Thou madest all days: this day Thou wast made of a woman, the Word WAS MADE FLESH. A pure virgin became a blessed mother; and Perfect God appeared as Perfect Man upon the earth.

LORD JESUS, Who this day camest down to me: Draw me up to Thee. Thou hast taken part of my nature: Unite me unto Thyself, and make me a true member of Thy Body. Make me partaker of the Divine Nature; save me from sinful stain; and make me wholly Thine for ever. Amen.

[*See Chapters* 52, 138, 139.]

122.—CIRCUMCISION.

O GOD, Who, for our example, didst cause Thy dearly-beloved Son to submit His pure and innocent body to the command of the law, and, for the encouragement of our hope, gavest Him the Holy Name of JESUS: Teach us, we pray Thee, with readiness and humility to obey Thy holy laws, and in all our need to call with joy and confidence on that most Holy Name. *Amen.*

LORD JESUS, most pure and holy: Have mercy upon me a sinner. Grant that the firstfruits of Thy blood may wash away the sin of my birth; and that the stream which flowed in the Garden and on the Cross may cleanse me from all my stains. Thanks be unto Thee for the laver of Regeneration in Holy Baptism, and for the cleansing grace of Absolution. Help me in purity and truth to obey Thy laws, and to walk in the same all the days of my life.

[*See Chapter* 113.]

123.—EPIPHANY.

O GOD, Whose Blessed Son was manifested that He might destroy the works of the devil, and make us the Sons of GOD, and heirs of eternal life: Grant us, we beseech Thee, that, having this hope, we may purify ourselves, even as He is pure; that, when He shall appear again with power and great glory, we may be made like unto Him in His eternal and glorious kingdom; where with Thee, O Father, and Thee, O Holy Ghost, He liveth and reigneth, ever one GOD, world without end. *Amen.*

O King of Glory, Who at Thy first coming hadst no palace but a stable, and no throne but a manger: Work in me an holy pride, and teach me to despise the world which so neglected Thee. Let the light of faith guide me all the way of this life, till I come to see Thee in Thy kingdom.

———

GOD, Who by the leading of a star, didst guide the Wise Men of the East in safety to Thy cradle, to worship Thee with gifts: Graciously remember me Thy servant, and guide me in all the places whither I go, with all speed, joy, grace, and peace, without any hindrance from adversity. And do Thou, our true Sun, our true Star, our true Light of Lights, Who didst lead them back, by the message of an Angel, to their own country; bring me again to my home, whole and unhurt, in all peace and safety and prosperity, by Thy succour, Who livest and reignest GOD, world without end. Amen.

———

124.—SEPTUAGESIMA.

LORD of mercy, in my grief I turn to Thee. I make no plea, but for Thy mercy. I have no claim to mercy, but my great need and Thy great love, and Thy precious promises. My soul, O gracious GOD, is weary of its load of sin. Father, forgive me all the evil I have done, and let the coming season of Lent be a blessing to my soul; for JESUS CHRIST's sake. Amen.

125.—LENT.
Penitential Psalms.

The Psalms called "Penitential" are *Psalms* 6, 32, 38, 51, 102, 130, 143. You will find it a good thing to add some of them to your devotions before and after self-examination or confession,—also on Fridays, in Advent and Lent, after falling into sin, and with the sick.

———

O let not my LORD be angry with me who am but dust and ashes. My sins cry for vengeance: can I cease to cry for pardon? LORD, silence them, or hear me.

I have broken Thy commandments: may I offer to Thee the sacrifice of a broken heart? Thou wilt not break a bruised reed; Thou wilt not despise a broken heart.

———

LORD JESUS, Thou didst hunger for our gluttony; Thou didst thirst for our drunkenness; Thou didst weep for our sinful laughter; Thou didst suffer torments for our delights; Thou didst die a shameful death for our shameful lives; Thou didst shed Thy blood for our crimson stains of sin. LORD, teach me to pray, and hear my prayers: teach me the evil of sin, and heal the wounds of my soul.

Let no sight please me, till Thy face shines upon me.

Let no sound delight me till Thy voice speaks peace, and says to my soul, I am thy salvation. Let me not enjoy sweet flowers and gardens, till I have gathered flowers from the Garden that was watered with Thy Blood. Let me pluck no pleasant fruit, till I have tasted of the fruit of the Tree of Thy Cross. Let me relish no food, till, with bitter herbs of sorrow and anguish of heart for my sins, I have prepared myself for my Easter Communion, and have received the Sacred Body and Blood of my Redeemer.

O JESU, Son of the Living GOD! most pure and without spot: Help me, that I be not occupied nor delighted with vain imaginations. Amen.

O JESU, Son of GOD! Who wast silent before Pontius Pilate: Restrain my tongue, until I consider how and what I ought to speak. Amen.

O JESU, Son of GOD! Who wast bound for me, govern my hands and all my members, that all my actions may be over-ruled for my good and Thy glory. Amen.

[*See Chapters* 35, 36, 37.]

126.—HYMN.

O LORD, on Whom alone I rest,
  Behold my failing heart;
And in the way Thou seest best,
  Thy healing grace impart.

The chains of sin have bound me fast,
  I cannot struggle free;
When shall my sorrows all be past,
  When wilt Thou comfort me?

Man cannot help me, nor relieve
  My bondage and my pain;
But JESUS came for me to grieve,
  For me my LORD was slain.

For me in love to earth He came
  To suffer and to die,
That I might live to praise His Name,
  With all His Saints on high.

When shall I see those wounds that Love
  For dying sinners bore,
And with the saintly throng above
  My Saviour's love adore!

O may I patiently endure
  While Thou dost leave me here,
And, while I struggle, make me sure
  That Thou art always near.

And make me know, O LORD, while now
  In desert lands I roam,
That, with Almighty yearning, Thou
  Dost long to bring me home.

O guide and keep me hour by hour,
  And bind my heart to Thee;
Protect me with Thy loving power
  From all that threatens me,

Where Thou Thy chosen flock
  dost lead
Make me content to go;
In thine own pastures let me
  feed,
Where living waters flow.

O LORD, in mercy hear my
  prayer,
Release me from my sin,
And day by day my soul pre-
  pare
The joy of heaven to win.

In JESUS' Name alone I plead,
  O grant the boon I crave,
In Him is all the grace I need,
  He liveth still to save.
[*See Chapter* 38.]   *Amen.*

127.—EMBER DAYS IN LENT.

The Ember Days at the Four Seasons are the Wednesday, Friday, and Saturday after—
1. The First Sunday in Lent.
2. The Feast of Pentecost or Whitsun-Day.
3. September 14.
4. December 13.

[*See Chapters* 144-149, 114 *Spring.*]

O GOD, the Pastor and Guide of Thy people. Look favourably upon Thy servants, who are to be ordained to any holy office in Thy Church; and guide them with Thy continual protection. Grant that, both by word and example, they may profit their flocks, and with them attain eternal life. Amen.

K 2

128.—HOLY WEEK.

LORD JESUS, may Thy yoke be sweet and Thy burden light to us through Thy Cross; that we may follow Thee cheerfully and come to the place where Thou art; for Thy mercies' sake. *Amen.*

LORD JESUS, write Thy wounds and Thy love in my heart—Thy Wounds, that I may hate the sins that grieved me,—Thy Love, that I may love Thee for that love.

129.—MAUNDAY THURSDAY.

O Sacred Feast! Wherein CHRIST is received; the memory of His Passion is renewed; our souls are filled with grace; and a pledge of eternal glory is given unto us!

Our Saviour and Redeemer, JESUS CHRIST, Who at Thy last supper with Thy disciples didst give Thy blessed Body and Blood under the forms of bread and wine: Grant us, we beseech Thee, ever stedfastly to believe and heartily to acknowledge Thine almighty power, and Thine infinite love towards us; and always worthily to receive the same Blessed Sacrament according to Thy holy ordinance; that Thereby we may obtain increase of all godliness in unity of spirit with Thee our Head, and by Thee and the Holy Spirit with all the company of them that are truly Thine — Thy spiritual and mystical body, and our spiritual and Christian brethren. Hear us, our Saviour CHRIST, for Thy Name's sake. *Amen.*

130.—GOOD FRIDAY.

Look Thou upon the wounds of Him Who hangeth; the Blood of Him Who dieth; the price paid by Him Who redeemeth thee. His Head is bent to kiss; His Heart is laid open to love; His Arms are set wide to embrace; His Whole Body is laid out to redeem. Think how great things are these; weigh them in the balance of thine heart; that He may be fixed whole in thy heart, Who for thee was fixed Whole upon the Cross.

LORD JESUS CHRIST, I see Thee lifted up, and mine eyes are turned to Thee. O let the spear that pierced Thee, fasten my heart to Thy Cross. Let the nails, that printed Thy hands and Thy feet, imprint Thy love in my soul. Let the thorns, that pricked Thy temples, not suffer the temples of my head to take any rest in sin. Let the vinegar, that was given Thee, melt my hard heart unto godly sorrow. Let the sponge, that was offered to Thee on the Cross, wipe out all the handwriting that records my sins.

Thou indeed hast borne our sins and carried our sorrows. Our heads devised wickedness: on Thy head was platted a crown of thorns. Our eyes burned with lust. Thine eyes were filled with tears. Our mouths uttered blasphemies: they spat upon Thy Sacred Face. Our bodies were stretched wantonly upon our soft beds: Thy Body was stretched upon the hard Cross. Our ears have listened to profaneness: Thine ears heard scoffs and cruel mockings. We have loved sweet odours: Thou wast led away to the place of a skull. We have sinned in gluttony and drunkenness: Thou wast offered vinegar mingled with gall. Our feet ran to evil: Thy feet were nailed to the Cross. Our hands were defiled with blood-guiltiness: Thy hands were stained with blood. Our hearts were pierced with the lusts of the flesh and the cares of the world: Thy heart was pierced with a spear.

Never were sufferings like Thy sufferings, because never was such a Sufferer. Never was sweat like Thy sweat, for never had any a burden like to Thine. Never were tears like Thy tears, because shed for them that thirsted for Thy Blood. Never were torments like Thy torments, because never was flesh so pure and tender as Thine. Never was sorrow like Thy sorrow, for none but Thee ever knew all

CHRIST of Saints and Angels' LORD!
This world's Light, in Heaven adored,
> Way and Truth and Life to all:
Peace and Health to every son
Whom Thy dying Love hath won,
> Man of Sorrows, Thee I call.

Seven Words from the Cross.
Seven words He spake, seven words of love; And all three hours His silence cried, For mercy on the souls of men; JESUS, our LORD, is crucified.

O LORD JESU CHRIST! Who, on the last day of Thy life upon earth, didst utter Seven Sayings, that we ought ever to have in remembrance: I beseech Thee, by the virtue of those Seven Sayings, to forgive me all that I have ever done or sinned in the Seven Deadly Sins, or in what proceeds from them—all my sins of Pride, Covetousness, Lust, Anger, Gluttony, Envy, and Sloth. Amen.

---

1. Father, forgive them! for they know not what they do. *S. Luke* xxiii. 34.
LORD JESUS, cause me, for the love of Thee, to forgive all that do evil to me. Amen. the source of sorrow and all the evil of sin.

2. To-day shalt thou be with Me in Paradise. *S. Luke* xxiii. 43.
Cause me so to live, that, in the hour of my death, Thou mayest so comfort my soul. Amen.

3. Woman, behold thy son! Behold thy mother! *S. John* xix. 26, 27.
Grant that Thy love may unite me to the fellowship of Thy Mother and Thy Saints, Thy Church and Thyself. Amen.

4. My GOD, my GOD, why hast Thou forsaken me? *S. Matt.* xxvii. 46.
So, in time of my affliction and tribulation, pity me a sinner, and help me; for Thou hast redeemed me with Thine own Blood. Amen.

5. I thirst. *S. John* xix. 28.
Grant that I may evermore thirst for and love and enjoy Thee, the Fountain of Eternal Light, with the devotion of my whole heart. Amen.

6. It is finished. *S. John* xix. 30.
Perfect Thy work in me, and prosper the work of my hands. Amen.

7. Father, into Thy hands I commend My Spirit. *S. Luke* xxiii. 46.
Thou hast set the bounds of my life. Go not far from me now; and receive me when I come unto Thee. Amen.

131.—EASTERTIDE.

O GOD, Who for our redemption didst give Thine only Son to the death of the Cross; and by His Resurrection hast saved us from the power of the enemy: Grant us so to die daily unto sin, that we may live with Him for ever in the joys of His Resurrection; through the same JESUS CHRIST our LORD. *Amen.*

May the Almighty Spirit, Who raised up JESUS our LORD from the dead, raise us from the death of sin unto the life of righteousness; that we may live in GOD'S favour, die in His peace, and rest in hope of a blessed Resurrection!

Glorious Sun of Righteousness, Victorious Redeemer, Who hast triumphed over the powers of sin and darkness, and conquered hell and the grave: Glory be to Thee, by Whom death is swallowed up in victory; Who by Thy glorious Resurrection hast made known the power of Thy Divinity, and proved Thyself the true Messiah, the beloved Son of GOD. Blessed be the power of Thy Birth in my regeneration, of Thy Death in the mortifying of my sin, and of Thy Resurrection in raising me from death to life.

LORD JESUS CHRIST, Author and Finisher of our Faith: Grant me to know Thee in the power of Thy Resurrection, enlighten my understanding, sanctify my will, moderate my desires, govern my affections, mortify my lusts, destroy the man of sin in me, and deliver me from this body of death. Work in me a fear of Thy power, a love of Thy goodness, a thirst for Thy grace, and a zeal for Thy glory.

132.—ROGATION DAYS.

The three Rogation Days are the Monday, Tuesday, and Wednesday before Holy Thursday, or the Ascension of our LORD.

O LORD and Heavenly Father, have mercy upon us Thy unworthy servants; and, though for our sins we have worthily deserved scarcity, sickness, and all evil; yet, for the sake of Thy blessed Son, and upon our own true repentance, send us plenty and healthful seasons; and grant that we, receiving Thy bounty, may use the same to Thy glory, the relief of those who are in need, and our own comfort; through JESUS CHRIST our LORD. *Amen.*

133.—ASCENSION DAY.

LORD JESUS CHRIST, Who art exalted above the grave in Thy Resurrection, above the earth in Thy Ascension, above the Heavens in Thy Sitting at the Right Hand of the Father: I praise Thee for Thy great humility; I rejoice with Thee in Thy exaltation; I wonder, when I see Thee become obedient unto death; I adore, when I see all knees bow to Thee.

I adore the mystery of Thy Incarnation; I tremble at the horror of Thy Passion; I exalt the power of Thy Resurrection; I exult in the glory of Thy Ascension. Thou wast born: so I am born again. Thou didst die for my sins: so I need not die in my sins. Thou didst rise from the dead: so my body may rest in hope of rising again. Thou hast ascended: so in my flesh I may see GOD, and enjoy the place prepared for me in Heaven.

Thou didst bless and sanctify the Earth by Thy Birth and Thy Life, by taking the nature of man formed of the dust of the ground; and by walking upon the earth, going about doing good. Thou didst sanctify the element of Water by Thy descent into the water of Jordan at Thy Baptism, and by walking upon the sea. Thou didst purify the Air, defiled by the fall of Lucifer from Heaven, by ascending triumphantly through the air into Heaven. And Thou hast even tried the Fire that tries all things; and hast made it pure, by the baptism of the Holy Ghost and of fire, even by sending down the Holy Ghost in the likeness of fiery tongues.

O LORD our Governor, how excellent is Thy Name in all the world! Creatures without voice praise Thee—the Heavens and the earth: without understanding know Thee —the Star that lighted the wise men: without will obey Thee—winds and seas: without ears obey Thee—the fig tree which Thou cursedst, and it withered: without natural affection mourn for Thee— the stones that clave, the veil that rent, the earth that quaked at Thy Passion: without will offer Thee service— the foal to bear Thee, the fish to pay tribute for Thee, the Sun to hide Thy shame, the cloud to veil Thee from mortal eyes and carry Thee up to Heaven. All Thy works praise Thee, and shall not Thy saints give thanks unto Thee? Let them tell the glory of Thy kingdom and talk of Thy power. For Thou makest the light Thy garment, the Angels Thy messengers, the air Thy pathway, the clouds Thy chariot; and Thou walkest upon the wings of the wind.

Thou art ascended up on high: Thou hast led captivity captive. In Thy Passion Thou wast the death of Death. In

Thy Burial Thou wast the grave of the Grave. In Thy Resurrection Thou wast the life of Life. In Thy Ascension Thou didst conquer conquest and lead captivity captive. LORD, may the gifts of Thy Ascension be granted unto me. Let my heart and desires rise up with Thee to Heaven. Ever fix my thoughts on Thee, Who art in Heaven; and on Heaven, because Thou art there.

LORD JESUS, breathe into my heart a most devoted love for Thee, contempt of the world, hatred of sin, longing for my heavenly country, and perseverance in penitence, which no evil desires may interrupt, until Thy compassion bring it to good effect. Amen. [See *Hymn*, p. 75.]

134.—WHITSUNDAY.

O Blessed Spirit, Who after the Father had manifested Himself in the work of Creation, and the Son in the work of Redemption, didst manifest Thyself in the work of Sanctification; appearing, as on this day, by the sound of a rushing wind and the light of fiery tongues: Manifest Thyself now to the Church, by enlarging her borders and making up her breaches; by hallowing her assemblies and preparing her ministers; by knitting the hearts of all her members in love, the bond of perfectness.

O Divine Fire, burning continually in the hearts of the faithful, and consuming all our spiritual sacrifices: Be a fire in my heart and tongue, that I may be fervent in my meditations and prayers, and zealous in the profession and defence of the truth.

Vouchsafe to be my Guide at all times and in all places. Remember me for good in my journey by Thy guardianship; at home, by Thy protection; in my prayers, by Thy help; in my afflictions, by Thy comfort; in my daily life, by Thy bounty; in my work, by Thy counsel; in my rest, by Thy care; and in all my ways, by Thy support.

Hymn.

Come, Holy Ghost, our souls
  inspire,
And lighten with celestial fire.
Thou the anointing Spirit art,
Who dost Thy seven-fold gifts
  impart.
Thy blessed Unction from
  above,
Is comfort, life, and fire of love.
Enable with perpetual light
The darkness of our blinded
  sight.
Anoint and cheer our soiled
  face
With the abundance of Thy
  grace.

Keep far our foes, give peace at home:
Where Thou art Guide no ill can come.
Teach us to know the Father, Son,
And Thee of both to be but One.
That through the ages all along,
This may be our endless song:
Praise to Thy Eternal Merit, Father, Son, and Holy Spirit.
[*See Chapters* 20, 21.]

135.—EMBER DAYS IN WHITSUNTIDE.

[*See Chapters* 127, 144-149, 114 *Summer*.]

136.—TRINITY SUNDAY.

All love, all glory be to Thee, O GOD the Father, Who hast made me and all the world.

All love, all glory be to Thee, O GOD the Son, Who hast redeemed me and all mankind.

All love, all glory be to Thee, O GOD the Holy Ghost, Who sanctifiest me and all the elect people of GOD.

Almighty and most wise Creator, Who hast made me; suffer me not to destroy myself.

Gracious Redeemer, Who hast come to save that which was lost: may I never lose my own soul, which Thou hast purchased for Thyself.

Blessed Spirit, Who dost sanctify the unclean: let me never defile what Thou hast made holy.

O Holy, Blessed, and Glorious Trinity, have mercy upon me. GOD of Heaven and Earth, turn my darkness into light; save me from Satan's thrall; heal my sickness; make straight paths for my feet; restore to me the joy of Thy salvation; grant me Thine inheritance; and crown me with Thy glory.

137.—EMBER DAYS IN SEPTEMBER.

[*See Chapters* 127, 144-149, 114 *Autumn*.]

138.—LITANY OF GOD INCARNATE.

GOD of GOD, for man decreed
To be born the woman's Seed,
Very GOD and man indeed.
　　Hear us, Holy JESU.

[*Repeat* "Hear us, Holy JESU," *after each verse*.]

GOD and man for evermore,
Who wast GOD with GOD before
There were creatures to adore.

Word, Whose wisdom all things planned,
Held by Whose Almighty hand,
All things in their order stand.

Son of GOD, when Adam fell,
Coming down as man to dwell,
GOD with us—Emmanuel.

JESUS, full of truth and grace,
Leaving Thine eternal place
To restore our fallen race.

Image of the GOD unseen,
Still what Thou hast ever been,
Though in form of infant mean.

GOD by Whom the worlds were made,
In a lowly manger laid,
Nourished by a lowly maid.

Long foretold in words divine,
Born of Royal David's line,
Yet what portion poor as Thine!

JESUS, led by love to share
All the forms of grief and care,
That we sinful mortals bear.

Good Physician, come to cure
All the ills that men endure,
And to make our nature pure.

Man of sorrows, weak and worn
With Thy woes for sinners borne,
Lest we should for ever mourn.

Saviour, bidding none to fear,
Gently bidding all draw near,
Who Thy loving message hear.

Shepherd, Who a watch dost keep,
Guarding still Thy chosen sheep
From the spoiler's malice deep.

Shepherd good, though hirelings flee,
Dying, that Thy flock may be
From the dread of dying free.

Holy of the holiest,
Source of blessing to the blest,
Of all teachers Prince and best.

Lamb, from earth's foundation slain,
By Whose bitter stripes of pain
We are freed from guilty stain.

Bearing all in sinners' stead,
Till Thy work was finished,
And Thy creatures saw Thee dead.

First from death in power to rise,
Bearing far beyond the skies
Thy prevailing sacrifice.

Only victim we can plead,
One High Priest to intercede,
Advocate in all our need.

Standing now before the throne,
Shewing that which can alone
For the sin of man atone.

Only hope of those who pray,
Only help while here we stay,
Life of those who pass away.
T. B. P.

139.—THE BLESSED VIRGIN.

Grant, we beseech Thee, O LORD GOD, that Thy servants may enjoy continual health of body and soul. Be ready to hear the prayers of the Blessed Virgin Mary for Thy Church. Deliver us from the sorrows of this life, and give us the enjoyment of eternal gladness; through JESUS CHRIST our LORD. *Amen.*

O LORD, we beseech Thee, stablish in our hearts the mysteries of the True Faith; that we may stedfastly confess him to be true GOD and Man, Who was born of the Virgin Mary; and, by the power of His saving Incarnation, may attain to eternal joy. *Amen.*
[*See Chapter* 52.]

140.—THE HOLY ANGELS.

O GOD, be favourable to me a sinner, and be my keeper all the days and nights of my life. May the Holy Angels and Archangels and all the company of heaven succour me! May my holy angel guardian give me help and strength, that no enemy may prevail to injure me in the way, by fire or by water or by sudden death, nor may hurt or destroy me waking or sleeping. And grant unto me so to be filled with the gifts of Thy Holy Spirit; that, going on from strength to strength, I may be enabled to attain to the happy society of the choirs of Thy Blessed Angels; through JESUS CHRIST our LORD. Amen.

141.—THE HOLY APOSTLES.

Almighty GOD, look we pray Thee, upon our weakness, and upon the burden of our sin which oppresses us. Hear the prayer of The glorious Apostles of our LORD and Saviour JESUS CHRIST, and grant that we may have strength to follow the confession of their faith; through JESUS CHRIST our LORD. *Amen.*

142.—THE HOLY MARTYRS.

Grant to us, Almighty GOD, that we, who know that Thy glorious Martyrs were strong in the confession of Thy faith, may have the joy of their fellowship in everlasting gladness; through JESUS CHRIST our LORD. *Amen.*

143.—FEAST OF ALL SAINTS.

[*The following Prayers may be used on the Feast Day of any Saint.*]

Patriarch and Holy Prophet,
  Who prepared the way of CHRIST:
King, Apostle, Saint, Confessor,
Martyr, and Evangelist.
Saintly Maiden, Godly Matron,
  Widows who have watched in Prayer,
Joined in holy concert, singing
  To the LORD of all, are there.

Almighty GOD, grant that we, who keep the feasts of Thy

Saints, may have a share in the communion of saints; through JESUS CHRIST our LORD. *Amen.*

Be pleased, O LORD, to hear the prayers of all Thine holy Saints; granting unto us both pardon of our faults, and also perpetual remedy for them; through JESUS CHRIST our LORD. *Amen.*

Most gracious GOD, the Author of all purity and the Lover of unity: grant that as Thy Saints pray to Thee for us, we may duly praise Thee for them, keep their feasts, and copy their virtues; till we all meet before Thy glorious Throne, and with one heart adore the Maker of us all; through JESUS CHRIST our LORD, Who with Thee and the Holy Ghost liveth and reigneth ever one GOD, world without end. *Amen.*

LORD, we pray Thee, of Thy great mercy regard the prayers offered unto Thee, and the aid granted by Thine appointment unto us Thine unworthy servants, by the ever-blessed Virgin Mary; by Thy Holy Angels, Archangels, Patriarchs, Prophets, Apostles, Evangelists, Martyrs, Confessors, Virgins, and all Thine elect servants; and grant us all that Thy love teaches them to desire for our help and salvation. Keep us, our Queen, and all Christian people in godliness; cleanse us from our vices; enlighten with heavenly virtues all that are joined to us by relationship and friendship, by religion and devotion; give us true concord and health; remove from us all enemies, seen and unseen; keep from us pestilence and famine; give charity to those that hate us; give health to the sick; direct the way of Thy servants in health and prosperity; and grant to all the faithful, living and departed, life and rest everlasting in the land of life; for JESUS CHRIST'S sake. Amen.

144.--THE CHURCH.
The Troubles of the Church.

O Almighty GOD, the Father of our LORD and Saviour JESUS CHRIST, Who hast brought us up as Thine own people, and hast led us all our life long unto this hour: We beseech Thee, of Thy goodness, to grant unto us that we may pass all the days of our life in peace and in Thy fear. Drive away from us, and from all Thy people, and from Thy Holy Places, all the craft of Satan, and all the counsels of wicked men, and all the assaults of our open and secret foes; and order all things by Thy Providence, as seemeth good and pleasing in Thy sight; through our LORD and SAVIOUR JESUS

CHRIST. Amen.
[*See Chapters* 59, 76.]

The Church of England.

O Heavenly Father, for my dear Mother, the Church of England, I, Thine unworthy child and hers, on bended knees, lift up my hands. Truth, love, and peace be with her. Hear, LORD, not the cries of our sins, but the sighs of her sorrows. Repair her losses, restore her rights, redress her wrongs; and grant her to shine forth in the beauty of holiness, to Thy glory, her honour, and our happiness; through the grace of our LORD JESUS CHRIST. Amen.
[*See Chapters* 60, 77.]

145.—PEACE AND UNITY.

Peace.

O GOD of Peace; Bless those that seek peace, that they may find it; stop and turn those that are enemies unto peace, that they may seek it. Bow their hearts to it that have the power: strengthen their hands for it, that have the will. As for those who set their hearts and hands against it, turn not Thy hand and face against them, but lead them to repentance. O forgive us the sins that deserve Thy wrath, and send us a peace that may preserve us in Thy fear; for JESUS CHRIST's sake. Amen.

Unity.

O GOD, the Father of our LORD JESUS CHRIST, our only Saviour, the Prince of Peace; Give us grace seriously to lay to heart the great dangers we are in by our unhappy divisions. Take away all hatred and prejudice, and whatsoever else may hinder us from godly Union and Concord: that as there is but one Body and one Spirit, and one Hope of our calling, one LORD, one Faith, one Baptism, one GOD and Father of us all, so we may henceforth be all of one heart and of one soul, united in one holy bond of Truth and Peace, of Faith and Charity, and may with one mind and one mouth glorify Thee; through JESUS CHRIST our LORD. Amen.

[*For* "*Peace and Unity,*" *p.* 103.]

146.—REVIVAL.

O LORD, revive Thy work! Breathe upon the dry bones, that they may live. Save Thy Church, which is Thy Body, and Thy Spouse. Keep her from all enemies seen and unseen. Uphold and maintain Thy Truth. Let not error and heresy corrupt it, ignorance hide it, superstition stain it, profaneness trample upon it, schism tear it, sacrilege devour it, unbelief deny it, persecution overcome it. Let error cease, sects vanish, the spirit of love and peace return. Bid confusion end, irreverence depart, holy order and decency be restored. So shall sinners be converted unto Thee, and Thy Saints rejoice in Thee. So shall we ever be giving Thee thanks, because Thou defendest us; for the glory of Thy Name, the quiet of our lives, and the salvation of our souls. Amen.

147.—SPIRITUAL GIFTS.

LORD, we see not our tokens. There is not one prophet more; neither is there one among us that understandeth any more. Thou answerest us not by dreams, nor by visions, nor by prophets. The sick are not healed; the lepers are not cleansed; the deaf hear not; the gospel preached unto the poor is not confirmed by signs following.

Our sins have separated between us and our GOD. Thou hast covered Thyself with a cloud, that our prayers should not pass through. Thou art far off, and goest not out with our armies, as in the days of old.

LORD of mercy, return unto us. If it be not Thy will that our sons and our daughters should speak with new tongues and prophecy for the conversion of sinners, nor that dreams and visions should direct the way of Thy saints— Thy will be done. Come unto us as Thou wilt. Only leave us not destitute of Thy manifold gifts. Deal not with us according to our sins, but according to Thy mercy; and let signs and wonders be done in the Name of Thy Holy Child JESUS. *Amen.*

148.—HOME MISSIONS.

LORD, have mercy upon us, and upon those who, by our neglect, are perishing for lack of knowledge in our own land. Give us grace to repent of our sin, and strength to amend. Prosper the efforts now made to bring back the sheep that have strayed from Thy fold. Save Thy flock from false doctrine, heresy, and schism, from hardness of heart and contempt of Thy word and commandment. Rebuke the evil spirit of pride, that we may submit our judgments and our wills to the teaching of Thy Church. Rebuke the unclean spirit of lust, that our hearts and all our members may be obedient to Thy laws. May our souls and bodies be so cleansed by Thy Holy Spirit, that we may faithfully serve Thee in the unity of Thy Church, through JESUS CHRIST our LORD. *Amen.*

149.—FOREIGN MISSIONS.

O Almighty GOD, Whose dearly beloved Son, after His

Resurrection from the dead, sent His Apostles into all the world to preach the Gospel to every creature: Hear us, we beseech Thee, O LORD, and look upon the fields now white unto harvest; bless those labouring for Thee in distant lands, and prosper their handiwork; send forth more labourers into Thy harvest to gather fruit unto life eternal; and grant us grace to labour with them in prayers and offerings; that we, with them, may rejoice before Thee, through JESUS CHRIST our LORD. *Amen.*

150.—FOR MYSELF.

I. GRANT me, gracious LORD, a pure intention of my heart at all times, and a stedfast regard to Thy glory in all my actions. Possess my mind continually with Thy Presence and ravish it with Thy love; that my only delight may be, to be embraced in the arms of Thy protection.

II. Be Thou a light unto mine eyes, music to mine ears, sweetness to my taste, and a full contentment to my heart. Be Thou my sunshine in the day, my food at the table, my repose in the night, my clothing in nakedness, and my succour in all necessities.

III. LORD JESU, I give Thee my body, my soul, my substance, my fame, my friends, my liberty, and my life; dispose of me, and of all that is mine, as it seemeth best to Thee, and to the glory of Thy blessed Name.

IV. I am not now mine, but Thine. Therefore claim me as Thy right, keep me as Thy charge, and love me as Thy child. Fight for me when I am assaulted, heal me when I am wounded, and revive me when I am destroyed.

V. My LORD and my GOD, I beseech Thee to give me patience in troubles, humility in comforts, constancy in temptations, and victory against all my spiritual enemies. Grant me sorrow for my sins, thankfulness for Thy benefits, fear of Thy judgments, love of Thy mercies, and mindfulness of Thy Presence for evermore.

VI. Make me humble to my superiors, and friendly to my equals: make me ready to please all, and unwilling to offend any: make me loving to my friends, and charitable to my enemies.

VII. Give me modesty in my countenance, gravity in my behaviour, deliberation in my speech, holiness in my thoughts, and righteousness in my actions. Let Thy mercy cleanse me from my sins, and let Thy grace bring forth in me the fruits of everlasting life.

VIII. LORD, let me be obedient without arguing, humble

without feigning, patient without grudging, pure without corruption, merry without lightness, sad without mistrust, sober without dulness, true without doubleness, fearing Thee without despair, and trusting Thee without presumption.

IX. Let me be joyful for nothing but that which pleases Thee; nor sorrowful for anything but that which displeases Thee. Let that labour be my delight, which is for Thee; and let all rest weary me, which is not in Thee.

X. Give me a waking spirit and a diligent soul; that I may seek to do Thy will; and, when I know it truly, may perform it faithfully, to the honour and glory of Thy ever-blessed Name. Amen.

151.—FOR MY FRIENDS.

For all my relations and friends, LORD, receive my prayers. Do good unto them all, O GOD.

To those that err shew Thy truth: those that seek truth keep from error.

Those that do evil help to do well: those that do well keep in the right way.

To those that are afflicted give comfort and relief: to those that prosper give humility and temperance.

Bless the sick with health: save the healthy from sickness.

Supply the needs of those that want: let those that want not supply the needs of others.

To all grant Thy grace, and shew Thy mercy. Let love bind us one to another, and unite us all to Thee; that we, who meet in this world, may not be parted in the world to come. Though we suffer and scatter on earth, may we live and love together in the bliss of Heaven; for JESUS CHRIST'S sake. Amen.

152.—FOR ALL MEN.

LORD GOD Almighty, merciful and pure: Be pleased in favour to consider the weakness of man; and so sanctify us with Thy grace that we may all confess our sins, and cry to Thee for pardon; all acknowledge our weakness, and cry to Thee for strength; all see our ignorance, and come to Thee for knowledge how to behave ourselves in this mortal life in our several callings; that Thou mayest be glorified for ever. Amen.

153.—THANKSGIVING.

Holy Trinity, Blessed and Adored for ever! To Thee—for Thine own perfections, and for Thy dealings with Thy whole Church, and with me a sinner, in time past, present, and to come—be all blessing, and honour, and glory, and power, for ever and ever. Amen.

www.ingramcontent.com/pod-product-compliance
Lightning Source LLC
Chambersburg PA
CBHW020258170426
43202CB00008B/422